ARMCHAIR INVESTING

Making Money in Stocks – *Simplified*

Aditya Shroff

www.visionbooksindia.com

www.visionbooksindia.com

Disclaimer

This book is the author's opinion about investment methods which he thinks are appropriate. These methods may or may not work for the reader. It is not meant to be an advisory to any person whatsoever. The author shall not be responsible for any losses which may arise due to the use of any part of the contents of this book, and readers are advised to take appropriate expert advice before investing.

First Published 2011
Reprinted 2012
Second Edition 2015
Reprinted 2016, 2020, 2022, 2023, 2024

A Vision Books Original

ISBN 10: 81-7094-916-5
ISBN 13: 978-81-7094-916-9

Published by
Vision Books Pvt. Ltd.
(Incorporating Orient Paperbacks & CARING imprints)
24 Feroze Gandhi Road, Lajpat Nagar 3
New Delhi-110024, India.
Phone: (+91-11) 2984 0821 / 22
email: visionbooks@gmail.com

Printed at
Ashim Print Line
38/2, 35 &36 Sahibabad Industrial Area, Ghaziabad
Uttar Pradesh 201010, India.

Credits

A humble thank you

To the Supreme God,
to my Guru Master Choa Kok Sui,
to my Mai and to all my teachers
for their priceless blessings.

Contents

Introduction

I have been an investor in stocks for the better part of my working life. Being a broker, analyst and fund manager myself, there have been ample chances to interact with various intermediaries, journalists, investors and fund managers. I enquired of several of them for a simple investment system which any investor could follow without getting out of his home or, figuratively speaking, getting up from his or her "armchair". But, alas, none could tell me a method to invest easily and sensibly. They spoke about Ben Graham, Peter Lynch, Warren Buffet and such famous personalities, and then asked me to read various books written by or about them. I tried, but found them too complex and difficult to follow.

All I wanted to do was to be able to invest some of my hard earned money in all those wonderful stocks which doubled and tripled in a year. So, left with no choice, through trial and error I put together my own method of investing.

Not being a big investor like Rakesh Jhunjhunwala, nor having the mental faculty of Udayan Bose and not having the time to see CNBC throughout the day, should I quit investing in today's topsy turvy financial world and put all my money in the hands of fund managers *via* the various mutual funds available in the market?

No! Emphatically not!! I discovered that investing is mere common sense and any individual can invest sensibly in the stock market. It is easily done and I shall guide you in your efforts to become a sensible investor.

Please note the key word is sensible and not sensational.

Lucky is the name of the fictional instructor in the book. Meghna and Akash are two typical, everyday fictional people to whom Lucky explains the Armchair Investing method in a simple and easy going manner. While the male gender has been used when referring to an investor in the book, it is also meant to include the female gender.

Anecdotes have been given in boxes at the end of various chapters. They have been arranged chronologically and help illustrate the armchair investment strategy.

1

Why Invest in Stocks?

Meghna: I want to become a successful and famous investor. What should I do?

Lucky: Stand in a queue! On a serious note, though, I cannot answer this question because I don't have the answer.

Meghna: No, no! I am very serious. Please teach me to be a great investor.

Akash: Me too.

Lucky: I can guide you to become a sensible investor. But first tell me why you want to invest in stocks and not in other conventional financial instruments, such as bank deposits, gold, real estate, and so on?

Meghna: My friends tell me that investing in stocks is very profitable. I feel that it's the more "in" thing. If I am good at the stock market, I can make a killing and spend the money on things I cannot afford now.

Akash: I have read this too, and feel that stocks give a better return than any other form of investment.

Lucky: Well, I agree with Akash, but would caution Meghna not to get too carried away by the glamour of stock investing. Though investment in stocks gives a better return than other forms of investment, it can be very hazardous to our capital if we are not careful. It is preferable that stocks be a part of your portfolio, and not be the only form of investment you do.

Akash: When you say part of your portfolio, what percentage of my portfolio do you mean? Some books say that this should vary with the age of the investor.

Lucky: That's a good query, and I shall answer that after I ask you a couple of questions.

The first one is — what is your perception of risk? This is more of a general question and relates to life as much as investment.

Akash: Risk means the possibility of losing something.

Meghna: Risk means not knowing the outcome of a situation.

Lucky: Okay, each of you has given a part of the answer. For me, risk is the loss which you may suffer in any situation when you have no control over the outcome, and the degree of risk depends on your lack of effort to steer the outcome in your favour.

Akash: Whoa! Explain that please.

Lucky: Take the example of driving a car. Let's say that you can drive a car and you set out in your car to go to office. Now, you do not know whether you will reach there safe and sound because the car may break down, or an accident may occur on the way. In effect, you have undertaken a venture with a risk by setting out to go to office in your car. The risk is that the car may break down or that an accident may occur. If you are a good driver, the chances of reaching without incident are much better than if you are a poor driver. The chance of a breakdown is the same in both cases. So there is risk in both cases, but the degree of risk is less if you are a good driver than if you are a poor driver.

Meghna: Well, that makes it easy to understand. You are saying that if we make the effort to learn how to invest, then we reduce our risk of losing money.

Lucky: Bravo! You have hit the nail right on the head.

Now to my next question — what is your stomach for risk, or how much risk can you tolerate?

Akash: You mean how much can I afford to lose?

Lucky: No, I mean how much can you afford to lose without losing any sleep over it! There is a difference. Some people can afford to lose a large amount of money and be unaffected by it, whereas others will get affected even if they lose a small amount.

So you should first decide how much money you can lose and still not be greatly affected. Then multiply that amount by three and you shall arrive at the amount you should invest in stocks.

Meghna: Why three times?

Lucky: Because as per my system you should generally be able to sell your investment before your lose one-third of the money you have invested. So your loss shall not exceed the amount which you have decided that you may lose and still not be greatly affected.

Meghna: But, then, every person may have a different level of loss that he can absorb without it really affecting him?

Lucky: Yes, this is subjective, and it must be decided before any investment is made. It can increase or decrease with experience, and may be reviewed from time to time.

With that, Akash, did you get an answer to your question about the percentage of your portfolio that you should invest in stocks?

Akash: What I understood is that you do not go by a percentage of the portfolio or the investor's age but by his risk tolerance. You also advocate that if we learn to invest, we can reduce our risk. Correct?

Lucky: Wow! You are a quick learner. Absolutely fantastic.

Meghna: And how do you compare investing in equity mutual funds with investing in stocks directly? Which is safer?

Lucky: I prefer investing directly, though investing through mutual funds may be a great idea if you cannot invest some time along with your money.

But there is one particular thing which should be clear in your mind when you are investing in equity mutual funds. The fund managers are paid to keep your money invested in stocks. They cannot and will not tell you to exit the fund even if they think the market is going to go down. They will simply try to invest in companies whose stock price, they feel, will fall the least. It is the investor's responsibility to exit when he feels that the market is over priced. So the answer to the second part of your question is no.

Meghna: But, then, the investor should understand that he has to take a call when to exit his investment. In most cases, investors don't take this call. Also, the financial advisors who sell the funds generally give the impression that investing in these funds is safer. If the investor does not know when to exit, will the financial advisor tell him?

Lucky: Ha! Don't be idealistic. He is not going to do any such thing. So it is better to do your own homework.

Akash: Yes, even I feel the returns are better in direct investment than in mutual funds.

Lucky: Okay, before we begin, tell me something about yourselves.

Meghna: I am a graduate in English and a home maker. I hardly read any newspapers but like to watch the news on television instead. I use the Internet for email and also use Facebook.

Akash: I am a Commerce graduate and an employee in a marketing company. I read the newspaper and watch some television, mainly news. I too access the Internet for email.

Lucky: Cool! You are more than qualified to become good investors. But you may need to spend some money.

Meghna: Money! How much?

Lucky: Relax. Only as much as it would take to subscribe to a couple of business magazines and a pink newspaper. That could be about two hundred rupees per month.

Akash: Thank God! I thought you would say a few thousands. I already buy the items you have mentioned.

Lucky: Okay, now on to the subject of investing in stocks. Do you invest in stocks at all?

Akash: Yes, I do, through a broker.

Meghna: And I invest in equity mutual funds. But I am not satisfied and want to do it myself. I am willing to work at it.

Lucky: Have you read any books on the subject of stock investing? Perhaps Peter Lynch's *One Up on Wall Street?*

Akash: No, I do not have the time.

Meghna: I really do not have the inclination.

Lucky: What about your mutual fund advisor or stock broker? Do they not advise you? What do you think of their advice?

Meghna: I think he is largely interested in selling his schemes. He claims to know a lot but I am not satisfied.

Akash: My broker is smart and once in a while gives good calls. But, then, he doesn't tell me when to exit.

Lucky: And now you want to know how to do it yourself?

Meghna, Akash: Yes.

Lucky: Okay, but my methods will not quadruple your money. These are simple but safe methods, and better safe than sorry is my personal belief.

Meghna, Akash: Let's begin!

Lucky: Great! Then we are all set.

Let us begin by understanding some financial terms and what they mean — quantitative factors; then some subjective terms — qualitative factors; and, then, some important concepts in investing.

The financial statements of any business comprises of three important documents — Balance Sheet, Profit & Loss Account and Cash Flow Statement.

Anecdote 1989

The year was 1989 and I had recently joined my father's stock broking firm. It had been a hard and volatile session at the stock market. I was having tea at a roadside stall, minding my own business, when this elderly gentleman, let's call him EG, approached me.

EG: You look tense, my son, what is the matter?

Lucky: It's nothing!

Obviously, I did not want to talk about it.

EG: I think the stocks you have purchased are troubling you, and you are questioning your decision about buying them.

How did he know that?

Lucky: Well, okay, let me admit that is one of the issues.

EG: And you are now faced with a decent sized loss.

Lucky: Are you some sort of a psychic?

EG: No, nothing of that sort. I have been through this before and know the symptoms. Can I be of some help?

Lucky: In what manner? I have bought the stocks and now I am making a huge loss. I should sell them as soon as possible to avoid making a bigger loss.

(Contd. . .)

Anecdote 1989 *(Contd.)*

EG: Ah! Hurry in buying and then hurry in selling, too! Typical nonsense I hear from young theoretical guys.

Lucky: Then what do you suggest

EG: Patience! Let me ask you how much time you spent before buying this shirt you are wearing?

Lucky: Fifteen minutes.

EG: Did you know that you wanted to buy a 100% cotton shirt with long sleeves, anti-wrinkle quality and blue stripes, or did you just decide on the spot?

Strange guy, I thought to myself.

Lucky: Obviously, I knew I was going to buy a 100% cotton long sleeve shirt. I decided on the pattern and quality on the spot.

EG: And how much time did you spend before buying your stocks? Did you plan that you were going to buy stocks today? Did you know the sector? Did you know the company?

Lucky: Hmm! Actually, I did not give it that much thought before doing so.

EG: So you planned when you had to buy a shirt worth ₹1,000, but not when you had to buy ₹3 lakh worth of stocks?! Is that not strange?

Lucky: You have a point there.

EG: Think about it.

(Contd. . .)

Anecdote 1989 *(Contd.)*

I was stumped to say the least but, after contemplating, found this to be true. When my trades were planned beforehand, I generally made money. But when investing on the spur of the moment, I took losses many more times.

Lesson: Research your investment.

1

Understanding the Quantitative Factors

2

Balance Sheet

Lucky: The Balance Sheet describes the financial status of a company on a particular date. It has two sides — Liabilities and Assets.

On the Liabilities side is listed what a company owes — to its shareholders, lenders, and outsiders.

On the Assets side is listed where the company has used its funds — whether in plant and machinery, investments, stocks, debtors and cash and bank balances.

The two sides must always be equal.

Meghna: Are there any specific terms used for the different sections in the Balance Sheet?

Lucky: Yes, in fact the terms are very specific, and by using these terms we can immediately know what is being spoken about.

Let us consider the Balance Sheet of a fictitious company, ABC Ltd. (***see*** Table 2.1). It will be easier to explain the terms using it.

Table 2.1

Balance Sheet of ABC Ltd. as on 31 March 20XX

		(Rupees in lakh)
Liabilities		
Share Capital:		
500,000 shares of 10 each		50
Reserves:		
Profit & Loss Account		40
Loans:		
Bank	20	
Term Lenders	15	35
Current Liabilities:		
Sundry Creditors	5	
Provision for Tax	3	8
		133
Assets		
Fixed Assets:		
Building	6	
Plant & Machinery	74	80
Investments:		
In subsidiary	7	
In Mutual funds	5	12
Current Assets:		
Stocks	20	
Sundry Debtors	12	
Advances	4	
Cash & Bank Balances	5	41
		133

The company ABC Ltd. has received money from its shareholders by issuing 500,000 shares @ ₹10 each to them. This money is called its Share Capital (₹50 lakh in the given example).

The company has conducted business to earn a profit. This profit, along with any other amount which belongs to the shareholders, comes under the broad head called Reserves (₹40 lakh).

The sum of Capital plus Reserve represents the shareholders' interest, or Shareholders' Funds in the company.

This sum divided by the number of shares issued gives the Book Value per Share (₹90 lakh divided by 500,000 or ₹18 per share).

The company has received loans, both short term and long term, from banks and institutions. These are called Borrowings or Debt (₹35 lakh).

The company owes money to certain people for products or services bought, and these are called Sundry Creditors (₹5 lakh). Taxes and other expenses payable come under Provisions (₹3 lakh). Collectively, these are called Current Liabilities (₹8 lakh).

Akash: Aren't these simplistic ways of describing important items?

Lucky: Yes. But then that's the point. Investing is simple and does not have to be needlessly complex at all.

Meghna: This is all too confusing. Please simplify it further.

Lucky: Well, that would take some doing!

Let's say that the Liability side comprises of all the money the company has to pay if it had to shut shop tomorrow.

Simply put, it is the money the company has taken from various people for the purpose of doing business.

Meghna: And where is this money used?

Lucky: For that we have to go over to the Assets side. This is the opposite of Liabilities. It shows where the company has used the money it has taken from various people.

The first classification is a broad one called Fixed Assets which comprises of all assets which can be used over a period of time, for example, land and building, plant and machinery, cars, etc. (₹80 lakh).

The company has made investments in subsidiaries and financial products. These are classified as Investments (₹12 lakh).

The company makes products, and the stock of products and raw materials is called Stock (₹20 lakh); the customers of the company who have purchased products and are yet to pay for them are its Sundry Debtors (₹12 lakh); the people to whom the company has given any advance or loans come under Advances (₹4 lakh); any funds lying with banks or as cash come under Cash & Bank Balances (₹5 lakh). Collectively, these are called Current Assets (₹41 lakh).

In all balance sheets, the total Liabilities equal the total Assets as they do in this case (₹133 lakh).

That gives a basic picture of the Balance Sheet.

Akash: That was nicely done. You have been able to cover the broad areas without making it cumbersome.

Lucky: Thank you, that was the aim.

Anecdote 1991

It was early 1991. Harshad Mehta was the reigning big bull of the Indian stock market, the king of all he surveyed. His favourite stock was ACC, trading near about ₹9,000 per share.

I had the following conversation with my grandfather, GF, a veteran of the markets for 60 years, and one of the oldest members of the Calcutta Stock Exchange.

GF: This man, Harshad Mehta, is making a fool of young boys like you.

Lucky: Why do you say that? He is smart and successful.

GF: He may be smart and successful but what he is saying is all rubbish. He is saying that the stock price of ACC is half of what it should be, whereas being a commodity producing company, the stock price should be half of what it is.

Lucky: The reason for his claim is that it would take so many hundred crore to make another company like ACC. Its current asset value indicates that the price should be twice of what it is now.

GF: The price of a stock does not depend upon its asset value unless the asset is being sold. The price depends upon the earnings of the company, and I do not think that ACC is selling itself or any of its plants.

Lucky: Grandfather, this is the new thinking.

GF: Whose thinking? You youngsters will soon find out the truth about Mehta.

What happened is now part of history. The world soon found out that Harshad Mehta was a fraud whose empire depended on stolen money.

(Contd. . .)

Anecdote 1991 *(Contd.)*

The lesson I took away is that sooner or later the market price will be a function of the earnings or earning capacity of a business and not its asset value, unless the company is going to change hands, or wind up.

Lesson: Price depends on earnings.

3

Profit and Loss Account

Lucky: The Profit and Loss (P & L) Account of a business pertains to the income and expenses of a business over a certain period of time, generally one year (remember, the Balance Sheet is only on a particular date).

The P & L Account includes all the income of a business. It also includes all its expenditure. The excess of income over expenditure is the profit of the business and belongs to the company's shareholders. This profit may be distributed as a Dividend and the balance, if any, may be transferred to Reserves.

Now, the Profit & Loss Account is the most important document of a business. It is based on this document that most investing activity takes place.

Meghna: Is that not supposed to be the Balance Sheet?

Lucky: Theoretically, maybe. But, practically no. A company may have a business with a great Balance Sheet yet have a poor Profit & Loss Account. Typically, in such a case you may find that its stock is trading at or below its Book Value. You may have a company with the reverse situation, and its stock price may be trading way above its Book Value because of its bright future prospects.

A great Profit & Loss Account can improve a bad Balance Sheet but a poor Profit & Loss Account will certainly make the Balance Sheet poor.

Akash: Now I understand why the market price of some stocks is below the Book Value.

Lucky: Remember you are always investing in the future, and that's most important.

As the Profit & Loss Account is a most important document, we shall discuss its headings separately with a small example.

Let's consider the Profit & Loss Account of the same imaginary company, ABC Ltd. (***see*** Table 3.1)

The term Sales (₹70 lakh) describes the amount received by a company from sale of its goods or services. It is interchangeably used with the terms "Turnover" and "Topline". It is the most important term in the investing dictionary. Sometimes, Sales is also described as Gross Sales and Net Sales. Gross Sales means the total sale value whereas Net Sales means total Sales less Excise Duty. In fact, this figure of Net Sales is more important than Gross Sales for calculation purposes. Whenever we use the term Sales in our calculations, we shall always mean Net Sales.

Table 3.1

Profit & Loss Account for the Year Ended on 31 March 20XX

		(Rupees in lakh)
Sales		70
Other Income:		
Interest on advance	5	
Sale of land	5	10
Total Income		**80**
Cost of Goods sold	25	
Other Expenses	8	
Total Expenses		**33**
Profit Before Depreciation, Interest and Tax		47
Depreciation	7	
Interest	4	
Profit Before Tax		36
Tax	6	
Profit After Tax		**30**

Akash: Why is this so important? Even more than the profit?

Lucky: The Sales figure tells us how much business the company is able to generate. Increasing sales tells us that the business is growing.

Meghna: But an increasing profit can also tell us that.

Lucky: You're right. It does. But an increasing profit, though important in itself, can also be because of other factors, such as a decrease in price of raw materials. Also, falling sales will generally spell doom for a company.

Profits are a function of how much extra consumers are willing to pay for the product but sales are a function of how many customers want the product.

Akash: Does it mean that an increasing sales figure is great?

Lucky: Yes. But not at the cost of profit. A great company achieves increasing sales while maintaining the profit margin.

Now on to the next headings.

Other Income (₹10 lakh) means income which is not from the business of the company. It can be from a regular source which is normal for the company to receive; for example, an interest on advances as in our example of ABC Ltd; or, it can be an extraordinary income which the company does not normally receive, as in the case of a sale of land in our example.

Meghna: How would we know the difference?

Lucky: It would be mentioned either in the accounts or notes to the accounts prepared by the company's auditor.

Akash: Okay, so the Sales plus Other Income would constitute the Total Income (₹80 lakh)?

Lucky: Yes.

The term Cost of Goods sold (₹25 lakh) is really self explanatory. This would include not only those goods purchased during the year but also those raw materials which were in stock with the company last year but were used this year.

Like the term Other Income, the term Other Expenses (₹8 lakh) includes all other expenses of the company, for example, advertising, travelling and so on. It also includes any extraordinary expense but not depreciation, interest and tax.

The term Depreciation (₹7 lakh) is the cost of wear and tear of machinery and is allowed as an expense in the Profit and Loss Account of any company. It is a notional expense and not an actual cash expense. The company would feel its effect only when it has to replace the particular fixed asset.

The term Interest (₹4 lakh) is the cost of outside finance used by the company for its business. This could mean long term finance taken from institutions and banks, or short term finance taken from its depositors, vendors and banks.

The term Tax (₹6 lakh) generally refers to Income Tax payable on the profits generated by the company.

Akash: But we see other terms mentioned, like PBDIT, PBT and PAT in the newspapers. What are those?

Lucky: Those are abbreviations used to describe the other headings in the Profit & Loss Account.

Profit before deducting Depreciation, Interest and Tax (₹47 lakh), or PBDIT, is calculated by deducting Total Expenses from Total Income.

Profit before Tax (₹36 lakh), or PBT, is calculated by deducting Depreciation and Interest from PBDIT; and Profit after Tax (₹30 lakh), or PAT, is calculated by deducting Tax from PBT.

Meghna: Which is the most important for us investors?

Lucky: For investors, PAT, also called Net Profit, is the most important. It is one of the defining terms for analysts all over the world. In fact, they use it to project the future price of an investment and we shall take advantage of that knowledge.

The term Net Profit describes the surplus of income over expenditure after paying all taxes. It is what the company does business for, and it belongs to its shareholders.

Akash: Do we use PAT for investment purposes? Is the PAT figure shown by companies always authentic?

Lucky: No, since PAT includes extraordinary income such as Sale of Assets, we deduct the extraordinary income from PAT to arrive at the Adjusted Net Profit. This is the figure which we should use for investment purposes (in our example, the Adjusted Net Profit is ₹25 lakh). Whenever we use the word Net Profit in our calculations, we shall always mean Adjusted Net Profit.

Sometimes unscrupulous companies inflate the PAT figure by putting false value to stock, or inflating the sales figure, etc. They do this for various reasons — to get higher loans, to raise money or to increase stock prices. So the figure may not always be correct. But good companies do not indulge in such manipulation.

Meghna: Then how can we know if the figure is correct?

Lucky: There is no way of knowing whether the company is inflating the figure but sometimes we can figure it out from the final important document of the financial statements of a company — the Cash Flow Statement.

Anecdote 1999

The year was 1999; I do not remember the month. My cousin, A, was a good player in the IPO business. (The IPO business deals with new issues of companies.) This conversation took place in his office.

A: Hi, Lucky! What are you doing in the market these days?

Lucky: Nothing much! My brokerage business is decent and my investments are performing well.

A: Buy shares of this company M! I am buying them in large quantities. I have got an insider tip from the management.

Lucky: I generally do not follow tips but, if *you* say so, I shall buy 1,000 shares.

I bought 1,000 shares at ₹80 per share. A week later:

Lucky: Bro, this tip has worked well. M is at ₹90 per share and I am making a good profit.

A: It will go to ₹120 per share. I have bought a large number of shares again during this last week.

Becoming greedy, I too bought another 1,000 shares, this time at ₹95 per share. A month later:

Lucky: Bro, the stock price had gone to ₹110 but now it is ₹85 again. What should I do?

A: I do not know who sold the shares to force the price down so much. The management also does not know. Anyway, do not worry about it. It shall turn out fine.

Being fearful, I called him up again after two weeks.

(Contd. . .)

Anecdote 1999 *(Contd.)*

Lucky: The price is down to ₹65 per share. I am feeling jittery and want to sell them.

A: Hold on for some time. I am speaking with the management.

Needless to say, I sold off my shares at a huge loss at ₹45 per share. But, unfortunately, A was ruined as the price went down to ₹15 per share. It was later revealed that the management had set him up. He lost his business and went through a particularly hard time in his life.

Lesson: **Do not act on tips and rumours.**

4

Cash Flow Statement

Lucky: The flow of cash is central to any business. The business collects cash from its shareholders, banks and other persons. It deploys this cash in plant, machinery and produces goods or services for sale; this sale of goods or services brings in cash which is used for further production, and so the process goes on. The statement which describes this flow of cash is called the Cash Flow Statement. This is divided into three parts:

1. Cash from operations;
2. Cash from investment activities; and
3. Cash from financing activities.

Meghna: How do we figure out whether net profits have been inflated from the Cash Flow Statement?

Lucky: The first part of the Cash Flow Statement — cash from operations — shows us the true picture. It tells us how much cash has been generated from the normal business activities of the company. It sets aside the clutter of financial jargon, such as Sundry Debtors, Diminished Stock of

Goods, etc., and tells us in a nutshell whether the company has been able to realize cash from its business or whether the company's cash is getting stuck in stock or debtors. The resulting figure may be very different from the net profit. While a different figure still does not confirm whether the net profit is inflated, it gives us an indication that something is amiss. The company would have to either show huge receivables or stock to inflate profits and this would be filtered out in this portion of the Cash Flow Statement.

Akash: Wow! And what do the other parts tell us?

Lucky: Cash from investing activities tells us where the company is investing its money — whether in subsidiaries or fixed assets; and the cash from financing activities tells us from where it's getting money apart from operations.

Together, all of these give us a pretty clear picture of what the cash flow of the company is about.

Akash: Is this what is meant by Cash Profit?

Lucky: No. In practice, Cash Profit is actually calculated by adding back Depreciation to Net Profit. The cash from operations could be substantially different from Cash Profit.

Meghna: Well, that would mean that this is an important part of the analysis.

Lucky: This is one of the most important parts of the analysis and one which you can ignore only at your own peril. And you will also learn how not to suffer even if you make a mistake. But we shall leave that for later. That brings us to the end of the financial statements of companies.

Meghna: That's it! You must be joking.

Lucky: I have never been more serious.

Akash: Can we learn to invest now?

Lucky: Ah! Not so fast. Now we shall understand some frequently used terms in the investing world.

Akash: I knew there was a catch.

Lucky: The first lesson to be learnt in the investing world is that there is always a catch. Things are rarely what they seem.

But anyway, let's go on. We shall learn about financial ratios.

Anecdote 2000

The month was December 2000 and I was discussing the stock market with the chief accountant of my firm. G was an experienced man, aged 65 years, and had seen many ups and downs in the market.

Lucky: G, what is your opinion of the market? It is strong. Do you think it will continue to go up?

I was confident that this old man was out of date and could not gauge the market in its computerized avatar.

G: I think the market will not sustain much longer. It must go down some time soon.

I was surprised but did not rebuke him out of respect.

Lucky: Why? Why should the market go down at all now? The government policies are pro-active and we have a rapidly developing middle class fuelled by the IT wave in the country.

(Contd. . .)

Anecdote 2000 *(Contd.)*

G: I do not know about that but I have been seeing that the group of bulls headed by Ketan Parekh has been paying an interest charge in excess of 36% to the market financiers. Till the prices were going up, he could afford to pay. But now that prices have been largely sideways for almost the full year, he may not be able to keep paying such usurious rates of interest. He had been going great guns as long as the market was bullish, and now the time to end this may be near.

Well, I did not act on this earthy piece of advice, but sure enough, less than two months later, the markets folded and so did the dreams of many investors.

It is very easy to be caught up in the heat of the moment. So, it is necessary to be able to gauge whether prices are in tandem with earnings, and whether a bubble is forming. An investor can do that if he is able to step back and analyze the market objectively.

Lesson: Beware of market bubbles.

5

Financial Ratios

Lucky: The first financial ratio we shall talk about is Operating Profit Margin, OPM in short. This describes a company's Operating Profit as a percentage of its Sales.

In the discussed examples of the Profit & Loss Account of ABC Ltd.,

OPM = (PBDIT – Other Income) x 100 ÷ Sales

= (47-10) x 100 ÷ 70 = 3,700 ÷ 70 = 52.86 %.

It is an important figure for assessing whether the company is outperforming its peers. In a comparison between companies, a higher OPM would indicate a better performance.

When comparing with past performance, an increasing OPM would mean more profits for the same turnover or, in other words, more bang for the buck.

Akash: So is a company with a higher OPM compared to that of a similar company in the same industry, better?

Lucky: Yes.

The next ratio is Return on Capital Employed, ROCE in short. This describes a company's Net Profit as a percentage of its Capital Employed (Shareholder's Funds plus Debt). Remember to use Adjusted Net Profit for all calculations.

In the same example of ABC Ltd.,

ROCE = (Net Profit – Extraordinary Income) x100
÷ (Share Capital + Reserves + Debt)
= (30-5) x 100 / (50 + 40 + 35) = 2,500 ÷ 125 = 20%.

Akash: What does this ROCE tell us?

Lucky: ROCE tells us how effectively the company has used the capital at its disposal. It tells us whether capital has been wasted or intelligently used.

Meghna: How would ROCE tell us this? Give us an example.

Lucky: Okay, that will make it simpler.

Let's say that a company, X Ltd., has a share capital of ₹1 lakh and it avails of a loan of ₹2 lakh. The total capital available to it is then ₹3 lakh. The company buys a second-hand car for its chief executive for ₹1.2 lakh, and uses the remaining ₹1.8 lakh for its business. Let's say it earns a return of 10% after costs on the money invested. It would earn ₹18,000 per year.

ROCE = 18,000 x 100 ÷ 3,00,000 = 6%.

If another company, Y Ltd., having a similar capital and loan, spends ₹60,000 on the car for its chief executive, and employs the balance ₹2.4 lakh for its business earning a similar return of 10% after costs, it would earn ₹24,000 per year.

ROCE of this company = 24,000 x100 ÷ 3,00,000 = 8%.

You tell me which company is more efficient.

Meghna: Okay, here the assets were similar but would the efficiency of the company not come down if it did not invest in appropriate assets? Maybe the profits would be lower because of the lack of investment in the required assets.

Lucky: True. Therefore the company must find a balance. It has to weigh the cost of such investment against the expected increase in profitability.

Akash: That's something! So, is a company with a high ROCE better than a company with a lower one?

Lucky: In most cases, yes. But then there are also other ratios to consider. This brings us to the third ratio — Return on Net Worth, RONW in short. RONW describes the Net Profit as a percentage of Shareholder's Funds.

In the same example of ABC Ltd,

RONW = (Net Profit – Extraordinary Income) x 100 ÷ (Share Capital + Reserves)
= (30-5) x 100 / (50+40) = 2,500 ÷ 90 = 27.78%.

This is the bottom line of the business, and it is the ratio I like best.

Meghna: Why?

Lucky: If the RONW of a company is greater than the return you achieve in your business, or greater than the return on any other investment where you can invest your money, then the company is doing a better job of deploying money than you are doing.

Now the Net Worth of a company (Share Capital + Reserves) divided by the number of shares issued by it gives us the Book Value per share, BV in short.

The Net Profit of the company divided by the number of shares issued by it gives us the Earnings per Share, EPS in short.

In our example of ABC Ltd.,

BV = ₹ (50,00,000 + 40,00,000) ÷ 5,00,000 = ₹18 per share.
EPS = ₹ (30,00,000 – 5,00,000) ÷ 5,00,000 = ₹5 per share.

We can restate:

RONW = Adjusted Net Profit*100 ÷ Net Worth %
= EPS x 100 ÷ BV % = 5 x 100 ÷ 18 % = 27.78%.

Akash: But then the stock price is often greater than the Book Value, so how do you compare your rate of return with that of the company?

Lucky: Great observation! You are learning fast! You can substitute the BV in the formula with the stock price and you will get the effective RONW with which to compare your return.

Let me give you an example. If the RONW of a company is 25%, and its stock price is two times the BV, then its effective RONW will be half of 25%, which is 12.5%.

Meghna: You've lost me. What's that again?

Lucky: Okay. Say you earn ₹10 for every ₹100 you invest and a company earns ₹25 for every ₹100 it invests in its business. But to buy one share of this company which has a

Book Value of ₹100, you have to pay ₹200. Then in effect you earn ₹25 for every ₹200. This means you earn ₹12.5 for every ₹100. Got it so far?

Meghna: Yes.

Lucky: Therefore you will compare your ₹10 earning capacity with this theoretical ₹12.50 and still be happy to buy the share at ₹200. Correct?

Meghna: Yes, it makes sense now.

Akash: Which would also mean that if my capacity to earn goes up, then the stock price I would be willing to pay will come down.

Lucky: Good observation again! Excellent!! This is why when interest rates on bank fixed deposits go up, stock prices tend to come down as people are less inclined to buy stocks. The reverse is also true.

This also means that when savvy investors feel that interest rates are on the way up, or down, they change their investment strategy accordingly.

Meghna: So if future interest rates are going to be higher than current interest rates, would it mean that savvy investors will begin to exit stocks?

Lucky: Yes. You guys are good!

But, then, more of this later. We are jumping the gun. There are some more financial terms to consider.

Anecdote 2001

The month was July 2001 and the markets were down after the Ketan Parekh fiasco. IT stocks were especially beaten down and IT sector mutual funds had been wiped out. I met a fund manager, FM, from Singapore.

FM: We have done extremely well in our funds. Our NAV has not fallen as much as those of our competitors.

Lucky: But the key word seems to be "fallen". Why could you not avoid the losses?

FM: We knew that the bottom would fall off IT stocks, so we bought stocks only of the stronger companies in that sector.

Lucky: If you knew the bottom would fall off, then why did you not sell the stocks and convert to cash?

FM: We cannot do so. We are given a mandate to buy stocks of a particular sector. We have to buy them.

Lucky: Is that the law?

FM: Yes, only a certain minimum percentage of the corpus may be kept in cash.

Lucky: Could you not wind up the fund?

FM: Does anybody do that? You just buy the best within the lot and keep the fund investors' money.

(Contd. . .)

Anecdote 2001 *(Contd.)*

That was the day I realized that people who invest in a mutual fund are actually taking a call to invest in the market at all times. The fund manager will remain invested even if he feels that the market will go down. He will not exit the market. The investor has to take that decision by selling his units. Therefore, if the investor has to take the decision, he had better be aware of what is happening in the market.

Lesson: **Even if you invest in mutual funds, you still have to make the final decisions yourself.**

6

Some Common Financial Terms

Lucky: The Face Value of a share is the value of each share when it is originally issued. This used to be ₹100 an era back. Now it is more likely to be ₹10, or even lower. The Share Capital is the product of the Face Value of the shares and the number of shares issued by the company.

Meghna: Why do some companies have a Face Value of ₹1?

Lucky: Generally, companies reduce the Face Value by "splitting" shares if the stock price becomes very high so that its shares may be bought by smaller investors. So a company whose share has a Face Value of ₹10 per share, can issue 9 fresh shares to each shareholder and thus reduce the Face Value to ₹1 per share.

Akash: Okay. Makes sense.

Lucky: A Dividend is what the company distributes to its shareholders out of the profits it earns. The dividend is always calculated on the Face Value of its share.

Akash: Many companies do not give dividends at all.

Lucky: Yes, that is the philosophy of some companies. They retain the dividend to re-invest that money in new ventures or in the expansion of business.

Akash: Then how do their shareholders receive any of the profits?

Lucky: Well, the promoters of such companies believe that the real profits of the shareholder comes from the appreciation in the stock price. But some companies do give out profits to shareholders in the form of Bonus Shares.

Meghna: What are Bonus shares?

Lucky: These are extra shares given free to shareholders in the ratio of their holding in the company. These shares are actually a form of profit distribution which is taxed only when you sell the bonus shares, unlike a dividend which is taxed immediately.

Let me explain with an example.

Let's say our company ABC Ltd. declares a bonus in the ratio 1:2. Each shareholder will then receive one bonus share for every two shares he holds. The total value of all the shares issued shall be reduced from the Reserves and added to the Share Capital. Now, only when the investor sells the shares does he pay tax on them. Till he holds the bonus shares, there is no tax. As per current law for Capital Gains tax, like any other shares if you hold the bonus shares for more than one year, you pay no tax at all when you sell them.

Meghna: Do you think it is right for a company to not give any dividends to its shareholders?

Lucky: Well, my opinion does not matter but as an investor I am looking for both — return as well as price appreciation.

So personally, I would definitely be happier buying the shares of a company which does give dividends and bonus, and also expands its business.

The Price / Earning Ratio, P/E ratio in short, is, as the name suggests, a ratio of the Current Market Price of the stock to the company's Earning per Share. It gives a quick way of understanding how expensive the stock is in relation to its earnings.

Akash: But we see that this varies hugely between industries and even companies within the same industry.

Lucky: Correct. It is also a measure of how much the stock is in demand with investors, and how the investors think that the earnings of the industry will increase in the future. Investors use this concept to project future prices based on estimated earnings.

Meghna: What do you mean? I have lost your thought process.

Lucky: The P/E ratio figure that you see in print is based on the historical earning. But savvy investors do not take into account only historical earnings when investing. They estimate the future earnings over several years, and then calculate an optimum price based on average P/E ratio for the company. After such an estimate is made, and the optimum price calculated, they buy if the current stock price is lower than this optimum price, or sell if the current stock price is higher than the optimum price.

For example, a company has earned ₹5 per share, and its price is ₹60 per share. Then the P/E ratio is 60 ÷ 5, i.e. 12. Now, a savvy investor would try to estimate the earnings of the company for the next year. Suppose his estimate is ₹7 per share after one year. He may calculate an optimum price of ₹84 per share after one year based on the same P/E ratio. Let us assume that this ₹84 per share after one year may be worth ₹75 per share in today's money after discounting. Discounting is a method of calculation of the current value of a future sum of money by using the current interest rate. This ₹75 is his optimum price today. Thus, for him, the current stock is cheap, and he will be a buyer.

So even if the P/E ratio seems high, it may not actually be so considering the growth prospects of the industry.

Akash: But then the investor could be very wrong in his estimate.

Lucky: Which is why stock prices rise and fall with every quarterly result, news, views and rumours as these affect the earnings estimate and, hence, the price at which the investor is a buyer or seller.

We now come to an important term we need in our arsenal of terms needed to invest effectively — Trailing Twelve Months, or TTM.

Wherever we have discussed the various terms so far, we used the latest audited results. But in reality we should use the figures for the previous twelve months ending with the last quarter. So if we have completed the December 2010 quarter, we should use figures for the year ending with the December 2010 quarter, i.e. from January 2010 till December 2010.

This has become possible in recent years as many publications and websites give this information which is based on the working of the company during the last twelve months. This concept is called the Trailing Twelve Months concept.

Akash: Why not just take the last quarterly results and extrapolate to twelve months?

Lucky: We should not do that because if the company has had a particularly good or bad quarter, we will draw wrong conclusions. Equally, we would get incorrect results for companies whose business is seasonal.

Meghna: Also, investing quarter to quarter may not be a good idea.

Lucky: Correct! But we are not going to ignore the quarterly results. We shall use both the quarterly result and the TTM results.

Meghna: Why the quarterly at all then?

Lucky: Because a large number of fund managers and investors out there re-assess their estimates based on such results. Also, we want to compare two corresponding quarters, meaning quarters which have ended on the same date in succeeding years.

We have been discussing quantitative terms with respect to a single company. But in reality one company may own one or more other companies. What then? The concept you should be familiar with regard to this situation is Consolidated results.

Akash: What's that?

Lucky: Many companies own more than 51% of other companies. Such other companies are called Subsidiaries, and the owner companies are called Holding companies.

The results of these subsidiary companies are added onto the results of the holding companies to give a true picture of the financial results of the holding companies. These combined financial results are called consolidated results.

Meghna: Why is it important to know about consolidated results?

Lucky: At times the subsidiaries themselves are so large that they can make a material difference to the results. Large investors use these consolidated figures when they make investment decisions. Therefore it becomes important for us to know them as well. It may so happen that a holding company has made a profit in one quarter, but when the results of the subsidiaries are combined with it, the sales and profit figures increase substantially.

Meghna: Can you give us a suitable example?

Lucky: Yes, of course, I can give many. Let us take a company like Hindalco. It owns the foreign company Novelis besides other smaller companies. Now Hindalco as a company shall declare two sets of results — one standalone, and the other consolidated. The consolidated results become very important because the size of Novelis is larger than that of Hindalco.

Akash: That makes sense. When do we go into investing details?

Lucky: In time. We have spoken about a large number of quantitative factors. Now we shall consider some qualitative factors about companies which have a direct bearing on our investment decisions.

Let me make it clear to you that our discussions will help you to invest effectively, but not make you fundamental analysts.

Now we shall talk about one of the most important, and oft neglected, areas of investment — qualitative factors.

Anecdote 2002

This is a conversation I had with a respected member, M, of The Calcutta Stock Exchange Association, Ltd. The month was October 2002, the markets were range bound and there was pessimism in the air.

Lucky: Good evening, sir! How are you?

M: Very well, and you?

Lucky: Quite okay. I am a bit confused though about a particular company and wanted your advice.

M: Go ahead, I shall help you as much as I can.

Lucky: The market for commercial vehicles has not been very good but I have heard from a friend that it is picking up. The largest company in this sector, Tata Motors, is in quite a bind. It had touched a low of ₹60 per share last year, and its Indica venture has not quite taken off as yet. For a commercial vehicle manufacturer, a passenger car seems quite a challenge. What do you think?

M: You are right in saying that it will be a challenge but I am sure that the company will pull through. You have to give due weightage to the management of the company and the Tata management being a good and honest one, will try their best to make the project a success. If you are satisfied with the other factors, then go for this stock and no other.

After speaking to the gentleman, I bought 1,000 shares of Tata Motors at ₹135 per share. It reached more than ₹900 at its peak in 2006. Their passenger car venture paid off handsomely, and now they have expanded overseas, too. It seems that sticking to a trusted management does pay off.

Lesson: **Always buy a good management.**

Understanding the Qualitative Factors

7

Management

Lucky: The most important qualitative issue which concerns us is the Management of the company in which we want to invest.

The term Management is the most important term in my dictionary. If the management of a company is a fair, transparent and effective one, the company can sail through good and bad times easily.

Meghna: Aren't the managements of all companies which have reached a certain level good?

Lucky: Let me explain this. The management of a company may be great, but they may not be fair to their investors. They may want to keep all the earnings for themselves and only give some dividends or a bonus to investors when they wish to raise additional capital in the form of a rights issue or a private placement. It is a fact that the management is only a trustee of shareholders' funds. But a large number of managements feel that the investor is a mere cash cow. They do not respect the rights of the shareholders.

Akash: But does the government not provide some protection?

Lucky: The protection for small investors is largely ineffective and this is the case not only in India but all over the world. The small investor is usually informed last about any event which affects the profitability of a company, and is left holding the can when companies go down.

Meghna: So this is why you rate management as the number one attribute?

Lucky: If I cannot trust its management, I do not invest in that company. Period!

Meghna: What about family owned companies?

Lucky: Generally, there is no distinction between professionally and family run companies. Family owned and run companies may have equally good managements. In fact, in a large number of cases family owned companies are run more efficiently.

Akash: How would you rate a management as good?

Lucky: Well, there are no set rules but one can get a good idea about the quality of the management by its past performance; the presentation of the balance sheet; the dividend and bonus record of the company; the reputation of the CEO and other board members; the media interaction by the top brass; the quality of the second rung of managers;

and from the stock market circles whether the management has a reputation for insider trading.

Meghna: What's insider trading?

Lucky: Insider trading refers to a case where some people in the management, or close to the management, indulge in stock trading based on sensitive information which they possess about the company and of which the public is not aware. This kind of trading is illegal in most parts of the world.

Akash: Why is the second rung of management important?

Lucky: This is so because it ensures that the top rung of management has ample support down the line, and also that the management is not concentrated in the hands of a few people. If the management is concentrated in few hands, the chances of manipulation of the accounts books are much higher.

Meghna: And what about past performance, bonus record, etc.?

Lucky: Companies go through good and bad times. Managements deal with these times in a manner which they think best. Good past performance shows that they have been able to adapt to different situations very well.

A good dividend and bonus record indicates that the management is probably investor friendly.

Akash: What type of managements do you generally avoid?

Lucky: Managements which have a reputation of wheeling, dealing and generally getting their work done by influence in political circles are some which I try to avoid.

Anecdote 2004

The month was November 2004. The markets were very bullish and every investor was making money except for me. I was sitting glum in my office when my brother, R, came visiting.

R: Hi, Lucky! How come you are in such a dull mood while everybody else is celebrating?

Lucky: Everyone is celebrating because the market is up, and I am glum because of that.

R: But why?

Lucky: The problem is that I got into the correct stocks and made a good profit. I sold them and was happy. Those very same stocks went up another 100% from there. Now, you tell me, should I be glum or not? I used everything I know about fundamental analysis to come to the conclusion that the stocks had become overpriced. But it seems that I was wrong.

R: Do you not know that prices depend upon perception of future earnings? Then why did you sell them?

Lucky: I took the anticipated earnings into account and even then found the stocks were overpriced, or so I thought.

R: Apparently not! So you are saying that fundamental analysis provided you with the right stocks to buy, but did not tell you the correct time to sell. Tell me, do you use technical analysis at all?

Lucky: No, I don't.

R: That is the only system by which you can get a proper exit.

Lucky: Do I have to learn something new? Now?

(Contd. . .)

Anecdote 2004 *(Contd.)*

R: Why not? You are never too old to learn. Do it and you shall thank me forever.

Well, I will indeed be forever obliged to my brother who introduced me to technical analysis. This laid the groundwork for my investment strategy.

I now routinely use both fundamental analysis and technical analysis.

The important lesson to take away from this incident is that one needs to learn and work hard to be a good investor. Fortunately, any one can do so, even with limited capital, and at any age.

Lesson: Never stop learning. Fundamental analysis and technical analysis are complementary.

8

Nature of Business

Lucky: We shall now consider the nature of a company's business. The business of a company can be basically classified into two types — commodity or non-commodity type of business.

Now, at this point let us give due respect to the great man of investment, Warren Buffet. This is one of his ideas. My salute to this great investor and philanthropist of the world.

A commodity type business is one where the product or service is price sensitive. For example, the airline business. Cheaper seats are easier to fill than those based on great service.

A non-commodity type business is one where the product or service is not price sensitive, which means it sells because consumers have a fancy for it. For example, the soft drinks business. Consumers prefer one to the other, and would be willing to pay some extra money for the one they like rather than switch brands.

Akash: Sounds interesting. What are the other general features of such businesses?

Lucky: The other feature of a commodity type business is that it is continuously trying to increase sales by lowering prices and introducing new products. To do so, it invests heavily in plant and machinery and other automated processes which suck out its cash. Remember, the competition is doing the same and, therefore, it's a constant battle for supremacy. The consumer has a good time switching between brands which offer greater value.

Whereas the other feature of a non-commodity type business is that it is cash rich, and whenever it gets a chance, it increases the price of its products which results in higher profits and a great positive cash flow.

Meghna: So, what do we take away from this?

Lucky: The simple fact that the chances of a non-commodity type business to succeed are far greater than those of a commodity type business. So wherever possible, we should try and invest in non-commodity type businesses.

Akash: I had really never seen it in this light.

Anecdote 2005

The IPO of Jet Airways came in 2005. There was excitement in the air and it seemed that investors would be well rewarded. My father, F, did not share my enthusiasm.

Lucky: Hi Dad, the Jet Airways IPO is now over and I think the stock is going to do quite well.

(Contd. . .)

Anecdote 2005 *(Contd.)*

F: I am not so sure. I remember the fate of Damania and East West Airlines. Jet Airways is a good airline, no doubt, but Indian Airlines is a public sector company. It has limitless funds available to it. Also, the business is very price sensitive.

Lucky: Why?

F: It is a dog-eat-dog business. Whoever offers cheaper seats is going to win. New airlines can enter the field easily. In fact, low cost airlines are coming up all over the world and it is only a matter of time before they arrive in India, too.

Lucky: So what? Jet Airways with its superior service will beat Indian Airlines hands down and also be able to fight any competition from newer airlines.

F: I have my doubts. Airlines all over the world are becoming more like commodity businesses. In fact, I hear that in New York, you can call up airlines and play them against each other for cheaper seats. They fall over themselves to give you benefits like free excess baggage and flyer miles.

Not really understanding what my father said, I bought 100 shares at ₹1,200 per share. Then I read a book about Warren Buffett's investment philosophy regarding commodity and non-commodity businesses and my father's advice sank into me. I sold the shares at ₹900 per share in 2007. In February 2009, the stock was trading at ₹130 — an erosion in value of nearly 90%. Since then other lower cost airlines like Indigo and Spice Jet have established themselves. The other full services airlines, Indian Airlines and Kingfisher Airlines, are also in dire straits.

Lesson: Buy non-commodity businesses.

9

Debt

Lucky: The next term is Debt. Debt is a four letter word but it is not something to abhor or be afraid of. We have spoken about Debt when we discussed Balance Sheets. (*see* Chapter 2). Here we do it with a qualitative perspective.

Again, let us pay homage to the great educator and author, Robert Kiyosaki, who in his books has presented a simple explanation of good and bad debt.

We have modified his version a bit to suit our investment needs.

Debt is good in the hands of those companies which can handle it well — which means those companies that have a very good ROCE and typically, which is higher than the cost of debt taken. Debt can be lethal for companies which misuse capital, and can prove fatal in a period of downturn in the economic cycle.

Meghna: So would you invest in companies having high debt but low ROCE?

Lucky: Those companies would be given a lower rating than others when we choose the company in which we want to invest.

Akash: So, this is not a disqualifying factor.

Lucky: No, none of the qualitative factors discussed previously, apart from management, is a disqualifying factor. They all need to be considered when comparing investment opportunities.

Akash: When you say economic cycle, what do you mean?

Lucky: We shall discuss that shortly.

Anecdote 2006

The month was July 2006. I was discussing an investment of mine with my wife, A.

Lucky: I am really disgusted at myself.

A: Why?

Lucky: I invested a large chunk of money in a company H. The company has some excess land which it was going to sell but the deal has not come through as yet.

A: So what? It will happen sooner or later.

Lucky: Yes, it may. But during this time I have lost some major opportunities to make good money. A blue chip company like Larsen & Toubro has jumped from ₹600 per share in March to ₹1,600 per share now in July; and here I am stuck with H. I had bought it at ₹150 three years ago and it is still stuck at ₹150.

A: So why did you not sell it earlier?

(Contd. . .)

Anecdote 2006 *(Contd.)*

Lucky: I tried but there was no buyer. The stock is completely illiquid.

A: Hmm. So what will you do now?

Lucky: I have been able to sell some of them in dribs and drabs, and have now resolved never to buy any stock which does not give me an easy exit.

It is the first criteria for any investment — exit. If an investment does not give a proper exit, it is better to stay away from it. This is the reason why we should buy only liquid stocks.

Lesson: Buy only liquid stocks.

10

Diversification and Expansion

Lucky: Diversification is, generally, something which companies do when they do not know what to do with all the extra money they have. It has often been seen that managements get a romantic notion of their invincibility when they are doing well, and venture into unrelated areas of business.

Akash: Why do you say generally?

Lucky: Because not all diversification is bad. Sometimes it is necessary to diversify in order to survive.

At times, diversification is confused with expansion. When a company expands into an area which will help its current business, or sets up a new plant to grow its current business, I call it expansion.

Meghna: So we should know why a company has chosen to diversify?

Lucky: Yes, and also whether the management team has the flair for the kind of business it is diversifying into.

Akash: But can the skills not be purchased in terms of manpower?

Lucky: Of course, this is what the management must do. The idea of diversifying for its own sake is not good, whereas diversification for the sake of survival is fine.

Akash: In a way you are saying that there is good diversification and bad diversification.

Lucky: Well, yes, you can put it that way.

Akash: Where do you think companies should expand?

Lucky: Companies should expand within their core competency and related businesses — both locally and in different parts of the world. No company can afford not to think globally in the current scenario.

We have now discussed a large number of quantitative and qualitative terms. Do you have any conceptual issues?

Akash: I do not have any issues but a comment. When markets are booming, unknown companies come into the limelight. They are spoken of in the media and some fantastic projections are thrown about. What do you think about investing in such companies?

Lucky: Generally, I stay away from unknown companies because I do not know their management. Nevertheless, we can check out the company and then take a call if it conforms to our norms.

Anecdote February 2007

The month was February 2007. The markets were bullish. I bumped into a friend, B, who I knew believed in fundamental analysis and thought that technical analysis was useless.

B: Hi Lucky, how is it going?

Lucky: Fine, and what about you? How is the market for you?

B: Doing well. I just bought some Infosys at around ₹2,000 per share.

Lucky: Okay, great!

B: Well, what do you think about it?

Lucky: I think it's on its way down technically so I would rather wait.

B: You and your technical analysis.

The month was October 2007. Markets were still up. I ran into this same person.

B: Hi Lucky, how are you?

Lucky: Fine, and what about you?

B: Doing well. Cannot understand though why Infosys is trading at only ₹1,800 per share. Everything is doing so well. Anyway, I bought some more.

Lucky: But it could go down even now.

B: It was looking good at ₹2,000. Now it's available at a lower price. The company is still doing well and, therefore, I averaged.

The month was December 2008. He called me.

(Contd. . .)

Anecdote February 2007 *(Contd.)*

B: Hi, Lucky? It's B.

Lucky: Hello B! How are you?

B: Not good at all. I just sold off my Infosys at about ₹1,200 per share.

Lucky: Why on earth did you do that?

B: I got tired waiting for it to go up. I lost a lot of money on it.

Lucky: But the chart looks as if it is bottoming out. I just bought some shares.

B: I don't know. Thanks anyway.

A couple of things struck me. One — averaging a loss making investment is not a good habit. Two — it is important to admit your mistake if the market is going against you.

Lesson: Never average a loss.

3

Important Concepts in Investing

11

The Economic Cycle

Lucky: Investment in stocks is one of the most important investment activities for any individual. This has been said many a time. It is true but for one small detail.

Stocks need to be entered into in a timely manner and carefully. They then need to be monitored regularly and, finally, you need to exit them at the right time, too. Otherwise, a large percentage of one's capital can we wiped out mercilessly. There is no government or institution in the world which can stop and reverse a falling market.

Meghna: Is there something you are trying to tell us by using those words?

Lucky: Yes. Please note the words — "entered into . . . timely", "carefully", "monitored regularly" and "exit . . . at the right time" in the last couple of sentences.

Meghna: What does "timely" mean?

Lucky: Timely means at the appropriate point in the economic cycle.

Akash: I've lost you there.

Lucky: Okay, I shall briefly explain the economic cycle. This is extremely important and will form the basis of all our investment decisions. Here I must pay tribute to Sam Stovall for his excellent work on Sector Investing, and Robert Prechter for his excellent work on Elliott Waves. This learning has been, in part, inspired from their work.

It has been seen over time that economic activity takes place in cycles. The period of these cycles can be as little as four years to as long as fifty years. But what interests us here is the four-year cycle. This cycle has different phases and we shall discuss the basic features of each phase so that you can identity the relevant phase easily. We should take pains to identify the phase in which we stand in the economic cycle because this will help us time our entries and exits.

The economic cycle consists of 6 phases. To make it simple, let's number these from 1 to 6.

- Phases 1 to 3 consist of a growing economy in its early, middle and late stages.
- Phases 4 to 6 consist of a declining or a contracting economy in its early, middle and late stages.

When an economy is growing, the media often describes it as a boom. When an economy is declining or contracting, the media often describes it as a recession.

It has been seen that not all sectors of the economy do well at the same time. They behave differently in different phases of the economy with some sectors doing well even in the declining phases of the economy. We look for such behaviour and try to identify the phase we are in. The characteristics of the various phases are:

Phase 1 or early stage of a growing economy: Business is growing again. Interest rates have bottomed out. People are optimistic. Salaries are showing signs of improvement, and jobs are again beginning to be available. Sectors which begin to do well in this phase are computer software, airlines and shipping.

Phase 2 or the middle stage of a growing economy: Every business looks as if it's booming. The economy is good, prices are rising, and people are spending freely. The general mood is one of success and well-being. Interest rates are rising. This is the real positive period of the economy. Almost all sectors are doing well, especially metals, coal, fertilizers, heavy equipment, engineering and infrastructure.

Phase 3 or the last stage of a growing economy: Some skeletons come out of a few cupboards. Prices become unbearably high. Interest rates, too, are very high. Mortgages have become expensive. Most people are talking about the stock market. Stock prices are volatile. Unknown, low priced stocks, also called cats and dogs, are coming into the limelight. In fact, some stock prices are falling. Growth is other stagnant or down. Sectors which are doing well are oil exploration, oil marketing and refineries.

Phase 4 or early stage of a declining economy: Suddenly, all stocks are falling. There are also more skeletons tumbling out of cupboards. There is some scam or the other in the financial markets. People are getting laid off. Jobs are scarce. Central banks and governments are trying their best to control inflation. Interest rates are peaking. Sectors which are doing well are defensive sectors, such as pharmaceuticals, cigarettes, food and household fast moving consumer goods.

Phase 5 or middle stage of a declining economy: Jobs are practically unavailable. Inflation is down. Interest rates are also coming down. People are expecting the worst. Investment advisors are expecting the bottom to fall off. Sectors which are doing well are gas, power, banking, loans and financial services.

Phase 6 or last stage of a declining economy: Some sectors begin to show improvement. People are beginning to talk of hope. Interest rates are still coming down. People are starting to spend on some durable products. There are some signs of revival. Sectors which begin to do well are auto, real estate, home appliances, consumer durables and textiles.

Akash: Okay, we get the picture, but then what is "timely"? How does this description of the economic cycle help in investing?

Lucky: "Entered timely" is getting into the stock market when the economic cycle is showing signs of revival, which is Phase 6 or Phase 1 of the cycle.

"Exited at the right time" is getting out of the market in Phase 3 of the economic cycle. This means selling our investments when the business cycle is at its peak. Maybe the prices in the stock market can go somewhat higher, but it is not wise to stay in the market right till the end. The mistake which many investors make is that they get wedded to their investments. They cannot bear to part with them. But this is not the sensible way to approach the market.

Meghna: How does one know in which phase the economy is in at any point in time?

Lucky: Fortunately, the stock market does that for us. As described above it predicts the economy better than any economist in the world. We should look for tell-tale signs of each phase. Analyzing these will give us a fairly good indication of the current phase.

Meghna: Okay, now what did you mean by "carefully" and "monitored regularly"?

Lucky: "Carefully" means to choose a stock after doing some homework; "monitored regularly" means following the stocks you are invested in on a regular basis. We shall talk about both a little later.

Anecdote December 2007

It was December 2007. The markets were at an all-time high. The BSE Sensex was at 20,000+ and all the experts were talking of 25,000. My uncle, S, dropped into my office for a cup of coffee. Now, he is a veteran of the stock market and is a pure fundamental investor.

Uncle: How is it going, Lucky?

Lucky: Never been better Uncle. The market is up and business is good.

Uncle: Are you speaking fundamentally or technically?

Lucky: Both, Uncle. The economy is buoyant and the charts are going through the roof.

Uncle: Hmmm! I think you may be in for a surprise quite soon.

Lucky: What sort of surprise?!

(Contd. . .)

Anecdote December 2007 *(Contd.)*

Uncle: I think the market is waiting to collapse.

Lucky: What?! Why do you say that? What is your basis for it?

Uncle: The P/E ratios of all shares are near their highs. If you have noticed, the IT and auto sectors have been down since early 2007. Now even capital goods are going down since October. The only sectors which are keeping your Nifty afloat are metals and oil. This is the classic ending of the economic cycle. You think about it.

This got me thinking and I went through all my investments with a microscope. I had not realized that the sectors he mentioned were in a fall mode. I quickly shifted my stocks to my List 13 (which we shall talk about later), and exited as soon as the market began to fall. I had made good profits and was able to protect them.

Lesson: Follow and monitor your investments closely.

12

Inflation, Money Flow and Behavioural Trend

Lucky: Let's now look at three more important concepts — inflation, money flow and behavioural trend. These are concepts which are often misunderstood or neglected. Entire books can be written about these but we shall study them only with respect to our stock investment strategy.

Inflation, as we all know, is a measure of yearly price increase in commonly used items. In India, this is announced by the government. Investors have somehow been led to believe that lower the inflation, the better it is for the economy. This is absolutely incorrect.

We need a healthy level of inflation to keep the economy's wheels moving. Let me explain simply.

If the prices of goods and services increase reasonably, the companies producing them make more profits. They are able to give higher salaries; employ more people and also go in for expansion. As employees take home bigger pay packets, they are able to spend more on themselves, thereby improving their standard of living. This earning and spending activity leads to growth of the economy.

When the inflation is extremely high, however, companies find it difficult to keep up with costs which rise disproportionately to the sales price of their products. As a result, business profits come down and companies are unable to pay better salaries or go in for expansion. The employees are able to buy less for the same pay packet and hence their standard of living comes down. The earning and spending cycle slows down and this leads to a contracting economy.

When inflation is very low, companies are not able to increase profits, salaries do not rise, and there is no incentive for capital expenditure. The earning and spending cycle stagnates and the economy goes into a decline.

Akash: So what is the best situation from an investment point of view?

Lucky: A healthy inflation rate, which is a little lower than the bank fixed deposit rate, is the best for the market and this is generally witnessed in Phase 2 of the Economic Cycle.

Related to this is a term called fiscal deficit. This is the deficit in the annual budget of the country and is measured as the excess of its expenditure over income. The government can do either of two things to cover this deficit — print currency notes or borrow. Either way, a high deficit means high inflation and is not good for the economy in the long run. A reasonable deficit is a good way to keep the economy buoyant and this should be the aim of all governments.

Let us go on to money flow. We shall not refer to the economic concept of money flow. Wherever we use this phrase, we are referring to its literal meaning — the flow of money.

It is known to all but not admitted by most governments that markets all over the world are dictated by gigantic institutions, banks, mutual funds and hedge funds — all flush with money. Whenever these institutions move into any market with their money, the prices of the assets traded in that market shoot up. Whenever these institutions move out of the market, the prices of the assets come down. At such times prices of the assets bear little or no relation to their intrinsic value and are, instead, a result of pure demand and supply.

In other words, big institutional players can make or break markets across the world with impunity.

Meghna: Where do these institutions invest?

Lucky: They may invest in any asset — stocks, bonds, commodities, currencies and real estate.

Meghna: So how does this affect us?

Lucky: We need to keep a track of where these large investors are investing. For example, we have heard about foreign institutional investors (FII) investing in the Indian stock market. This is a common indicator of money flow from outside India into the Indian markets. Simply said, if money is flowing into the stock market, it is likely to rise. If money is flowing out of the market, it is likely to fall.

Meghna: Is that the reason why TV channels flash the FII investment figures so often?

Lucky: Yes.

Akash: Would this situation repeat itself in all markets, such as gold, silver, etc.?

Lucky: Yes, it would.

Akash: So, are you saying — follow the money?

Lucky: Yes! You got it.

Okay, now on to the last concept — behavioural trend.

Behavioural study is a study of human behaviour in different situations. It has been concluded that humans react and behave irrationally to situations in certain circumstances. I shall speak of only one aspect of this science — herd instinct.

We have often heard the term — herd mentality. Generally when one uses the term, one is referring to a set of people who behave in the same manner, irrespective of the rationality of such behaviour. This is entirely true, especially in the stock market. At times of very high stock prices, investors seem to lose their common sense and behave irrationally by buying stocks at very high prices which have no relationship to their worth. In fact, they disregard all prudent advice and even urge their friends and relatives to follow their example. There is uncommon euphoria and hope all around. This phenomenon is also referred to as a bubble.

Akash: Even I have noticed this. The so-called experts give bullish calls even at the peak of the market, and bearish calls at the very bottom.

Lucky: Yes. And we are going to take advantage of this by our own disciplined approach to stock investment. When we feel there is euphoria, we shall exit; and when we feel there is extreme pessimism, we shall enter.

Akash: Wow! This is phenomenal.

Anecdote 2008

The month was January 2008. The market was at its peak with the BSE Sensex at 20,000+ levels, and this was just before the bottom of the market fell off. I met an old uncle of mine, K, after almost four years. I knew that he invested in stocks in a small way.

Lucky: Uncle! Good to see you after such a long time. How come you are here in Kolkata?

K: I have come to attend the wedding of my friend's daughter.

Lucky: Great! Your daughter, too, I think, is of the age. When will she get married?

K: Son, I do not have the funds right now but I am going to rectify that situation soon enough. I am going to buy Reliance and sell off my Hindustan Lever.

Lucky: Why uncle?!

K: My friend had bought shares of Reliance about five years ago. He sold those now to get the money for his daughter's marriage. I have shares of Hindustan Lever which I have kept for the same purpose. This is my favourite stock but it has not appreciated much in this bull market.

Lucky: What are you saying Uncle? This bull run has been the best India has ever seen.

K: I know, son, but it is my bad luck.

(Contd. . .)

Anecdote 2008 *(Contd.)*

Lucky: Uncle, you should not buy stocks now because the market looks overpriced.

K: No, no! I must.

Saying this he went away. I shudder to think what must have happened to his investment. He was married to his favourite stock and now he was going to get married to his friend's favourite stock. Buying stocks just because they have paid us well in the past is not smart investing. Past performance is no guarantee of future performance.

Lesson: **Do not marry your stock.**

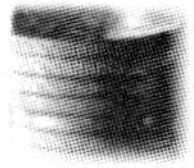

13

Investment Rules and Tools

Lucky: Investment in stocks is the most profitable kind of investment for anyone. I advocate a simple common sense based investment method. Anyone following this method will be in as comfortable a situation as the best of investors out there.

There are some basic investment rules all investors must follow:

1. **Never argue with the market.** If it's going up, there is probably a reason for it. If it's going down, there is probably a reason for it. Most of the time we shall not be able to explain its movement. Our ignorance is vast and we should not pay for it with losses.

2. **Never buy in a falling market.** Always buy a rising market. Always buy strength. In a strong market, always buy quality stocks — the best performing companies in the best performing sectors.

3. **Buy only liquid stocks.**

4. **Never average a loss making investment.**
5. **Never buy a share just because it is cheap.**
6. **Never underestimate the power of your own knowledge and study.** We can spot a lot of things much before professionals do because we are not presumptuous. Never stop learning. Have total self belief.
7. **Do not believe rumours, never follow tips or hot stocks.** There are enough stocks out there which can give us a great return. Do your own homework.

Meghna: Wow, let's get down to business. What tools shall we need?

Lucky: The only tools we need are:

1. Website of NSE — www.nseindia.com (*see* Appendix A);
2. Website of the Bangalore Stock Exchange — a web portal which also provides content, news, corporate financial data — www.bgse.co.in (*see* Appendix B);
3. A business magazine which gives us financial data of companies sorted by industry — *Capital Market* (*see* Appendix C);
4. A website which provides technical charts — www.icharts.in/charts.html (*see* Appendix D);
5. A business newspaper, such as *The Economic Times* or *Business Standard.*

Akash: How should we use tools like websites, magazines, newspapers and electronic media like television?

Lucky: We need to use these resources for information and news about the state of the economy, industries and companies. We should try to increase our awareness of products which companies manufacture, the major raw materials they use, the major markets where they sell their products, their plans for diversification and expansion; the vision of the management, and also be able to find out if they are in trouble.

Meghna: What about experts' suggestions to buy or sell stocks of companies? Should we listen to them?

Lucky: We should evaluate their suggestions using our own methods but not follow them blindly.

Akash: Is it really that simple?

Lucky: Yes, it is. No analyst can make money for us. It is our disciplined approach to investment which will enable us to do so.

Anecdote January 2009

Early in the trading session on 7 January 2009, Satyam Computer crashed from ₹180 to ₹35. The CEO, Raju, had confessed to embezzlement. The next day it crashed further from ₹35 to ₹10 before closing at ₹20. The following is a conversation with a friend, C, a week after that event.

C: Boss! I got hammered in Satyam.

Lucky: Why did you ever buy it?

C: It seemed so cheap at ₹100 per share. I thought that the whole thing about Raju's confession was a hoax and that the price would bounce back.

Lucky: The fall in price was no hoax. The man is a crook.

C: But how could one know that from before? All the analysts were saying that the company has got ₹5,000 crore in its kitty. They were recommending buys on the stock at ₹175.

(Contd. . .)

Anecdote January 2009 *(Contd.)*

Lucky: You should know better than to believe the analysts on TV. They almost always speak on the correct side of the market. Satyam had recently gone from ₹120 per share to ₹180.

C: Yes, but tell me how would I have known? You have a strategy. How would the company have fared in your test?

That got me working. Satyam was not on my Main List (*see* Chapter 16) and I tried to run it through my investment factors again. It almost got through except on one count — promoter's stake. I got back to C with the results.

Lucky: Satyam sailed through my investment factors except promoter's stake.

C: What's that?

Lucky: I need all promoters of large companies to have at least 15% stake in the company. The Satyam promoter Raju had a stake of only 8%.

C: What does that mean?

Lucky: It would mean that he did not have a stake large enough for me to be convinced about buying the stock. Moreover, he sold the majority of his stake between October 2008 and December 2008. So had an investor kept track, he would have known that something was wrong.

C: Wow! I wish I had known and followed your strategy. Is it complicated?

Lucky: No, it is not. And you should follow it in future.

(Contd. . .)

Anecdote January 2009 *(Contd.)*

It seems from the Satyam story that there will always be rich promoters who are dishonest. As investors, we have to be aware of this and take adequate precautions.

Lesson: **Look for a decent promoter's stake.**

■ ■ ■

Anecdote March 2009

It was March 2009. The markets were improving a bit after the huge downtrend throughout all of 2008. This uncle of mine, S, who has featured in the December 2007 anecdote, came into my office to have a cup of coffee. Naturally I look forward to his visits as his nuggets of wisdom have always helped me in the past.

Uncle: How are you, Lucky?

Lucky: Good, Uncle. Stocks are looking up but the economic news is not so good. What do you think?

Uncle: Markets have been at these levels for a long time and I think the worst is over. The economic news is mixed at worst and you may be seeing a revival.

Lucky: Do you think I should buy some stocks? Which ones?

Uncle: Which are the sectors you prefer?

Lucky: Those which have been battered in this fall. Like realty, infrastructure and capital goods.

Uncle: What about auto and IT?

Lucky: Are you suggesting these? What is your basis for it?

(Contd. . .)

Anecdote March 2009 *(Contd.)*

Uncle: If the economy is reviving, these are the ones which should do best at the beginning of the economic cycle. In fact, their better performance during the past few months is the basis of my view. There is an old saying, "Always buy strength".

This got me thinking and I researched the auto and IT sectors and thereafter bought some stocks of the best companies in those sectors. They went on to their all time highs in the next few months. The ones I did want to buy — capital goods and infrastructure — also did well but not well enough.

It is not necessarily a good practice to buy those stocks whose prices have fallen the most. In fact, they have fallen because the companies are fundamentally weak. Even if these outperform the markets for some time, they will not do so in the long term. It is safer to buy stocks which are strong. Invariably, they will be the ones to perform better in the long run.

Lesson: Buy strength.

4

The Armchair Investing Set-up

14

Preparing List 1 With Quantitative Factors – Annual Data

Lucky: Let's begin by understanding that the method we shall discuss is not necessarily the best or the only method available. It is not implied that the companies in which we choose not to invest are bad companies. It only means that our money and time are limited.

The entire exercise involves choosing companies in which we wish to invest and constitutes the "carefully" part of the system.

Meghna: Okay, we understand, and we'll not hold you responsible for our losses.

Lucky: Thank you for your kindness.

We shall begin with the companies included in the CNX 200 index of the National Stock Exchange. This list has 200 of the top companies of the Indian stock market covering a wide spectrum of industries and representing over 89% of the market's total capitalization.

This list is available on the NSE website — www.nseindia.com (*see* Appendix A).

Akash: But we may miss out several good companies in this manner.

Lucky: Our aim is to make reasonable money with least risk. If we begin with the CNX 200 (also loosely referred to as the NSE 200), we are making sure that we shall be investing in the relatively bigger companies. These provide ample opportunities to make money. Yes, a lot of companies will be missed out but that is the price to pay in order to invest with discipline. As you become a mature investor, you may use the CNX 500 if you wish. Also, if there is an interesting company which is not in the CNX 200, the same rules may be applied, and if the company qualifies, it may be included.

The financial factors that we will use are — Annual Sales, RONW, and, then, Annual Sales again.

This information is available from the Corporate Scoreboard section of the *Capital Market* magazine, or the website of Bangalore Stock Exchange Ltd. (www.bgse.co.in) on the relevant Company Info pages — Income Statement (for Sales which is also in places referred to as Operating Income) and Ratio Analysis (for RONW).

We follow a simple system of eliminating those companies which do not fulfill our criteria. The steps are as follows:

1. First we classify the companies into large, medium and small based on their latest sales figures. Companies whose sales are higher than ₹5,000 crore are called large companies; those whose sales are between ₹1,000 crore and ₹5,000 crore are called medium companies; and those whose sales are between ₹200 crore and ₹1,000 crore are called small companies (*see* Appendix A).

We shall eliminate all companies whose sales are less than ₹200 crore.

There may be very interesting companies which will get eliminated under this criterion. In fact, a lot of these eliminated companies may have great investment stories attached to them. But for every ten great stories, there may be ninety disappointments; hence, we shall avoid them all.

2. Then we consider the RONW. The value of the RONW for the latest financial year should be greater than 10% for large companies, greater than 15% for medium companies, and greater than 20% for small companies, respectively. If the RONW is less than these prescribed figures, we shall eliminate such companies.

   The reason for using these rates is simple. Whenever we are investing money, we are incurring an opportunity cost and also taking a risk. We need to be compensated for both. As a PSU bank fixed deposit rate is approximately 8% over different periods, we shall consider this as the opportunity cost of our money. The balance is the compensation for the risk we are taking. Since the risk increases as we invest in smaller sized companies, we need to be compensated more for investing in them. Hence, the increased rate of RONW prescribed for medium and small companies.

3. The last figure we look at is sales. Generally, we shall use Net Sales which means Gross Sales less Excise duty paid. This figure should maintain, or grow, but not reduce. In the *Capital Market* magazine, there is a column within the Full Year columns called "Sales Var%". This compares the latest year's sales with that

of the previous year's figure. This should be equal to or greater than 0. If this figure is less than 0, it means that the Net Sales have fallen in the latest financial year when compared to the previous financial year and we shall eliminate such companies from our list.

If the *Capital Market* magazine is not available, then we can note the Net Sales or Operating Income figures for the current year and the corresponding previous year from the website www.bgse.co.in. The current year's figure should have either remained the same or increased from the corresponding previous year's figure. If not, the company is eliminated from the list.

The reason for looking at a maintained sales figure is that if a company can maintain its sales, especially during bad periods, then it will surely experience good growth during good times. Also, this factor would work well in all phases of the economic cycle. In case we are unable to get Net Sales figures, we can use figures for Gross Sales.

The resultant list is called List 1. Once List 1 is ready, we may note the Face Value, Management, Book Value, OPM and ROCE of each company to be used later for comparison.

Akash: What if a large number of companies are eliminated this way?

Lucky: The reason we do this is that we want to eliminate companies which have not performed in the immediate past financial year.

Meghna: Wow! But then a lot of popular companies must be getting eliminated as well. Will it take too much time?

Lucky: It can be done very quickly — a fraction of what it takes you to buy a new shirt or dress at the shopping mall, a few hours at the most.

Akash: Should we use standalone or consolidated figures?

Lucky: Generally standalone figures do the job which we are intending to do. If the consolidated figures are available from any website or your broker, you may use them as well. In case they are not easily available, it should not really pose a problem in the majority of the cases.

Meghna: How often should we review the list?

Lucky: You should review the list every quarter, in the third week of February, May, August and November as most of the quarterly results are out by then.

Now we are ready for the next round of elimination.

15

Preparing List 2 With Quantitative Factors – Current Data

Lucky: We continue with the elimination system in the second round and begin with List 1. In this round, we want to see how the companies have performed in the TTM and the latest quarter.

The best place to see these is the Corporate Scoreboard section of the *Capital Market* magazine. In case it is not available, then you can ignore the TTM and carry on with quarterly results alone. These can be obtained on the website www.bgse.co.in on the Quarterly page of the Company Info section.

The steps are as follows:

1. First we compare the TTM Net Profit with the corresponding figure for the previous year. It should have maintained or grown but not fallen. In the magazine, there is a column within the TTM columns called "NP Var%". This compares the current TTM Net Profit

figure to the corresponding figure of the previous year. This should be equal to or greater than 0. If the figure is less than 0, it means that the TTM Net Profit has fallen, and the company is eliminated.

2. We do a similar comparison of the latest Quarterly Sales and Net Profit with that of the corresponding period in the previous year. Within the Latest Quarter columns, there are two columns called "Sales Var%" and "NP Var%". Compare the current Quarterly Sales and Net Profit figures to the corresponding figures of the previous year. Both should be equal to or greater than 0. If either of the two figures is less than 0, the company is removed from the list.

   If the *Capital Market* magazine is not available, then we can note the Net Sales (or Income from Operations) and Net Profit figures for the current quarter and the corresponding previous year's quarter from the website www.bgse.co.in. Both the current figures should have remained the same or increased from the corresponding previous year's quarter figures. If not, the company is removed from the list.

3. The last parameter is the figure for the Promoter's stake in the company.

   It is required that the promoter's stake in all large companies be greater than 15%. There are several large companies with no identifiable promoter — these are professionally run and owned by institutional investors. We shall not eliminate such companies as per this rule; for example, ITC, Larsen & Toubro, HDFC Ltd. and ICICI Bank.

For medium and small companies, the promoter's stake should be greater than 25% and 35%, respectively. This information is available in the *Capital Market* magazine and the website www.nseindia.com under the Shareholding Pattern page of the Corporate Information sections. If a company does not meet the norm, it is removed from the list.

Akash: But then there could be a large number of companies which will not meet these conditions.

Lucky: Yes, but then it is essentially a qualifying process. It also means that fewer companies will remain on the list as we progress towards the end of Phase 3 of the Economic Cycle. These same companies will again begin to qualify once Phase 1 of the Economic Cycle begins.

Meghna: Why don't we compare TTM Sales?

Lucky: Excellent question. We avoid comparing TTM Sales because a surge in sales in one quarter of the previous year may result in the elimination of the company in this year. This is a situation we don't want. Whereas the effect of a similar situation of an unexpected windfall profit in a previous year is eliminated by comparing Adjusted Net Profit instead of Net Profit.

Akash: So actually we are comparing figures on several levels to eliminate companies as the economic cycle progresses towards the end of the upward cycle, and then include them again when the economy revives.

Lucky: Exactly. We compare the audited results, TTM and the latest quarterly result with the corresponding figures of the previous year.

Meghna: What if the current figures are less than the previous year's corresponding figure by a few crore?

Lucky: We are not finicky about a few crore here and there. What are a few crore between friends?! But, on a serious note, use your discretion in such cases. If the other figures are fine, then one figure off by a few crores really does not matter.

Meghna: Why are you so insistent on a high promoter's stake?

Lucky: There have been instances where the promoter has sold off his stake and then committed fraud. There have also been instances where the promoter has pledged his shares, and the lender has sold off these shares in the market. For our safety, we want a high promoter's stake in the company so that he will work in its best interests.

Akash: Is it possible that we are left with a very small list, and not have enough investment opportunities?

Lucky: Yes, it is, especially during recessions. And, hence, to our list we shall add all the stocks which are part of the CNX Nifty but which have been eliminated. The CNX Nifty which is popularly called "Nifty" comprises of 50 of the largest and most popular companies in India. The list is available on the NSE website.

Meghna: Why should we add them back?

Lucky: There are two reasons:

First, generally these companies are huge, and in tough times they do not meet our criteria but provide great investment opportunities at such times.

And, secondly, the stocks of these companies are in huge demand by foreign and large investors as these companies are the truly world class Indian companies.

Meghna: May we consider BSE indices as well?

Lucky: I was in the habit of using BSE indices earlier but have switched to NSE indices as the BSE does not disclose the constituents of its indices freely. It has become a paid service. The NSE indices do the job equally well.

Akash: So we are assured of at least 50 companies which belong to the CNX Nifty in which we may invest?

Lucky: Not really. The list of companies after addition of the CNX Nifty eliminated companies will consist of at least 50 and more companies, however, this will be called List 2, and all of the companies on this list have to go through the next round of elimination.

Akash: Oh, so you mean there is more?

Lucky: Yes, there is a third and final round of elimination which is based largely on the qualitative factors we have discussed earlier (*see* Chapters 7 to 10).

16

Preparing the Main List With Qualitative Factors

Meghna: There could still be many companies in List 2!

Lucky: There will be, in spite of the pretty stringent conditions we have used in the elimination process, especially in Phase 2 of the Economic Cycle. So we will go on further. The various steps in the third round of elimination are:

1. Our first qualitative criterion, as you may have guessed, is management. Companies, where we do not trust or do not know enough about the management, are eliminated. It does not mean that the management is bad. It is just that we are not comfortable with it because of some reason or because of plain ignorance.

   Unfortunately, this cannot be taught. It is more a matter of "feel" when we read about them and their interviews in business newspapers, magazines and see them on television. But the good part is that while we are not aware of this, we know enough of them in our daily lives through their charismatic leaders, products and brand names. For example — who does not know or has not heard about the Tatas, Birlas, Ambanis or Mahindras? It is very difficult to avoid the Maruti car, Airtel mobile phone or Hamara Bajaj. One is bombarded with advertisements of Lux and Rin. These famous personalities, products and brands which we see, hear about or use in our daily lives gives us an ample list of companies in which we may invest.

2. Companies whose business is commodity type are eliminated. But, remember, some companies whose business may appear commodity type command a good reputation amongst their peers based on the quality of their product, and hence acquire a non-commodity type flavour. These we retain. Let's consider an example — low cost airlines. The general nature of the business is that the customer will buy the cheapest ticket available at any point in time. But over a period of time some company may develop a reputation of cleanliness or timely service, and hence a customer may pay a bit more for flying in it rather than travel in its cheaper competitor. Such a company's business has gained a non-commodity type flavour.

   It may be remembered that if we cannot make a distinction between companies on this point, it is better to let the company remain on the list on the strength of the management than eliminate it because we are not able to distinguish the nature of its products *vis-a-vis* the others available in the market.

   In case List 2 does not comprise enough companies, we may avoid eliminating the companies based on this point altogether.

3. Companies whose business is glamorous, complicated, non-transparent, government policy dependent, labour intensive are eliminated.

4. We avoid companies which have a very high P/E ratio because generally these high prices are a result of excess euphoria, or some rumours, or a pending asset sale. If these rumours turn out to be unfounded or the asset sale does not take place, then the stock prices shall fall the most. It is better to be safe than sorry.

5. A company with a higher OPM indicates better performance, high ROCE indicates better efficiency, and high RONW indicates better returns. We would like to choose companies with higher OPM, ROCE and RONW amongst their peers.

6. Last, if a company is included in the popular indices like CNX Nifty (also called Nifty), CNX Nifty Junior and CNX Midcap, it is more desirable to invest in that company. The lists are available on the website of NSE (www.nseindia.com).

Remember, we began our list with the companies in CNX 200, but those companies are also included in other more popular lists belonging to NSE. By comparing the companies on our list with each other based on their being on these already popular lists, the chances for safer returns increases with companies on the more popular lists *vis-a-vis* companies on less popular lists.

Meghna: Suppose I am suggested a company whose management is unknown to me, what should I do?

Lucky: First, run it through the quantitative factors. If it qualifies, then enquire about the management from your broker, friends and on the internet. Look at the popularity of its products. Read through its website. Look up its dividend and bonus record. Generally, a good management will have good dividend and bonus records. This information would usually be available on its website. If you are still unable to satisfy yourself about the investor friendliness of the management, either invest only a small sum of money in it, or simply stay away from the company and do not invest in it. There are plenty of other fish in the sea.

Akash: Why don't you like companies in glamorous businesses?

Lucky: Generally I find that the P/E ratios of such companies are too high for my liking. When I can get a better deal with other companies, why should I go in for these?

Meghna: What about government owned companies and labour intensive companies?

Lucky: Government owned companies are fine. In fact, some PSUs, as they are called, have done very well in the past few years. We avoid companies where the profitability may be drastically affected due to changes in government policies; and also those labour intensive companies where political decisions may over rule economic considerations. Basically, you can say that we avoid predictable uncertainty.

Akash: Should not any good company be worth investing in? What has being part of a popular index got to do with investment?

Lucky: It has a lot to do with it. Remember that you will make a profit only if someone buys your investment at a price higher than what you paid for it. There are umpteen stocks which can qualify even with our strict standards but their price fails to rise because they are not popular.

By following our method, we shall try to bring the list down to about 2 to 3 large, 1 to 2 medium and 1 to 2 small companies in each of 10 to 15 industries. If the number is fewer than this, it is no problem at all. In fact we can expect the number to be the highest in Phase 2 and to subsequently come down in Phase 3 of the economic cycle.

This is our Main List.

Meghna: So these are the ones you buy. Do you think this is enough? How much time will all this take?

Lucky: This number is good enough. The time you will take to make this list is only a few hours. So do it on the weekend, and you are on your way.

Akash: Great. Is there any more?

Lucky: Now let me ask you that if someone suggested the name of a company which you should invest in, what would you do?

Akash: Simple. I would see if that company is on my Main List, and if it is, then I would consider buying it.

Lucky: Yes, that is the way. Alternately, you can go through the company's figures using these same factors. If they conform, then you can add it to your list.

Meghna: You mean buy it?

Lucky: No, I mean add it, because there are certain other methods to be followed before you buy the stock. We shall talk about these later.

Now that we have discussed the "carefully" part, we come to the "monitored regularly" part.

17

Keeping Track

Lucky: Once the Main List is ready, two things need to be done to satisfy the "monitored regularly" part. These are:

1. First, this list has to be reviewed every quarter, after most of the results are out. A new Main List has to be made. This new Main List would include some new companies while some poor performers from the previous Main List would have been eliminated.

2. Second, some price data has to be maintained. We record the monthly closing price of stocks of all companies on our Main List. The closing price is the last figure in the price column against the name of the company in the market section of any business newspaper. For our purpose, we can use the closing prices on the last Friday of the month, which will appear in the next day's edition of the newspaper. Then we calculate the percentage price change from the previous month's recorded price so we know which companies are performing best, and which companies are performing better than the general market. The general market per-

formance is signified by the percentage change in CNX Nifty within the same period. We can conclude that a particular sector is outperforming the market if almost all companies within that sector are performing better than the general market. Now we already know which sectors perform better in different phases of the economic cycle (*see* Chapter 11). When we compare the outperforming sectors with this list, it will give us a valuable hint about the phase of the economic cycle we are in.

This may easily be done on an Excel or similar spreadsheet. On the sheet we can put the name of all the companies on our Main List sorted by industry. Then we record the closing prices of all the stocks on the last Friday of the month and calculate the percentage change.

Let's consider an example given in Table 17.1.

Table 17.1: **Determining outperforming sectors**

Main List					
Name	*Industry*	*26/6/2009*	*31/7/2009*	*Change*	*Change (%)*
CNX Nifty	Index	₹4,375.50	₹4,636.45	₹260.95	5.96
Hero Honda	Auto	₹1,406.20	₹1,605.30	₹199.10	14.16
Maruti Suzuki	Auto	₹1,059.25	₹1,414.45	₹355.20	33.53
ACC	Cement	₹799.10	₹880.80	₹81.70	10.22
Ambuja Cement	Cement	₹91.75	₹108.50	₹16.75	18.26
Infosys	Software	₹1,827.10	₹2,064.35	₹237.25	12.99
TCS	Software	₹397.40	₹525.95	₹128.55	32.35
While the index has increased 5.96% over the month, the clear winners are the Auto and Software sectors. This also signifies that we may be in Phase 6 or Phase 1 of the Economic Cycle.					

Akash: Please explain the purpose of the review exercise. What happens if a company in which we have invested does not make the grade any more?

Lucky: Generally, we do not pay much attention to what a company is doing if the stock is performing well. Also, we tend to get caught up in rumours, tips and hot profit stories from our friends, the media and brokers. The common refrain after losses occur is that "such and such person told me to buy this stock but he did not tell us when to exit". We need to have our own backup to avoid such situations. By such a quarterly review of the Main List, we can easily ascertain if our company continues to maintain its performance, and we can also run any recommended company through the same factors to evaluate a fresh purchase. In this manner we do not need to blame anyone else for our mistakes.

By the same yardstick, if a company no longer qualifies it means that its performance story may have paused or reversed, and it has to be deleted from the list and its shares sold off as per rules.

Meghna: How much time do you think this will take?

Lucky: A couple of hours per week.

Akash: Should we keep a daily track of prices?

Lucky: It is really not required for investors to do so. But it can be done, if we want to book some profit. I will tell you how to do this later.

Meghna: What if we choose a stock as per this process? When do we get out?

Lucky: Good question. You are now referring to the "exit at the right time". This will become clear to you a little later.

5

The Armchair Investing Strategy

18

Fundamental Strategy

Lucky: The golden rule of investment is to invest, and remain invested, only so long as you feel that the economic conditions six months ahead are going to be better than they are today. For this, do pay close attention to the general features of each phase of the economic cycle as explained earlier (*see* Chapter 11).

You must never go against this rule. There are no exceptions and this rule is inviolable. We do have a safety net in case you are wrong in judging the phase of the economic cycle so we need not worry too much on that score. But in case we feel that the cycle will be downward some time hence, there is no excuse to buy or hold shares of any company against this feeling.

You will develop this "feel" as you grow better informed and more aware of the economy. The stock prices of companies within certain industries will also serve as a warning.

Akash: Should we not book profits even if we feel that the economy is going to continue to grow?

Lucky: If you feel uncomfortable at any point in time, it is always a good idea to book profits and to take your money off the table. You can exit partially, or totally. Remember, even if you exit totally you can always step back, re-assess your position and invest again. Your comfort level is paramount because mental pressure will make you take wrong decisions.

Meghna: What if we feel that the economic conditions will be fine six months ahead, but some sector may not do well?

Lucky: Excellent question! Really you guys exceed my expectations. If you feel that any sector may not do well, avoid that sector. In fact as time goes by, you will be able to assess which economic factors are going against the future performance of companies within a sector. If the future seems bleak, there is no way we shall make money in that sector.

Akash: Please give an example.

Lucky: Let us assume that the RBI says that it may increase interest rates going forward. All those sectors whose profits may be hit should be avoided, for example the Automobile and Real Estate sectors, where a large proportion of sales depends on consumers getting cheap loans. Naturally if the interest rate goes up, the number of people willing to take loans to buy the products of companies in these sectors will become less, and consequently sales, profits and share prices will suffer.

Meghna: What if we are unable to assess the impact of such economic conditions as we are new to investing?

Lucky: The investing strategy which we shall discuss ahead should generally take care of this by itself. In other words the market will tell us where to invest our money.

Okay, now let's go ahead.

There are two parts to our investment strategy — fundamental and technical. The primary method is based on fundamental analysis, and the secondary method is based on technical analysis.

The primary method is quite sufficient to choose the stocks in which to invest. But the secondary method is used for confirmation and timing to enter and exit.

The fundamental strategy is as follows:

1. Once the Main List is ready, we shall maintain a chart of the monthly closing prices of the stocks of all companies on the list and calculate the absolute change and percentage change in price.

2. We try to keep track of the phase of the economic cycle. This can easily be done from the price chart where it is evident which sectors are doing better, and then correlate that information with the general characteristics of the different phases. For example if, month after month, the stock prices of the capital goods sector companies are increasing more than stock prices of those in other sectors in percentage terms, you may assume that we are in Phase 2 of the economic cycle. Please do note that general economic conditions have to confirm the indications being given by the price data. Also, the price data of one month is not enough. The pattern should continue for several months.

3. All investments shall be made in accordance with the signals received from the technical strategy.
4. Exposure in any one sector is limited to 10% to 15% of the portfolio. So the investments will be in at least 6 to 8 different sectors.
5. In any single sector, we shall allocate 70% or more of the funds to stocks of large companies and 30% or less to stocks of medium and small companies combined.
6. This carries on till we are in Phase 3 of the economic cycle. It is then time to become extra careful and look for signs to exit. A general sign is that while making the Main List afresh, the number of companies on the list becomes smaller each time a fresh list is made.
7. We can usually know how a company's stock price is performing relative to a benchmark index such as the CNX Nifty by comparing the percentage change in monthly closing prices of the stock with that of the index. If we find that for 2 or 3 successive months, the stock is performing better than the index, we can label the stock as an out performer. Conversely, if we find that the performance is comparable, we can label the stock as a performer; and, if we find that the performance is worse, we can label the stock as an underperformer. Naturally, we want to buy the outperformers.
8. If a stock in which we have invested has become an underperformer, we should consider booking profits in that stock.
9. All investments shall be made as long term investments. We shall call the list of all investments as List 55. But, in special situations (as will be described), some in-

vestments shall be treated as short term. We shall call that as List 13.

10. We may shift the investments from List 55 to List 13 in the following special situations:
    - When we want to book profits in a particular stock;
    - In Phase 3 of the Economic Cycle, or when we feel jittery about the market, or in "times of uncertainty"; and
    - When we wish to treat any investment as a short term investment.

    When we speak of "times of uncertainty" we mean that we are unable to ascertain the phase of the economic cycle at that time, and feel jittery about the market. This will be seen especially in the beginning of Phase 1 or near the ending of Phase 3 of the economic cycle, when the signals from the media and market may be confusing, and hence, we may want to treat our investments as short term.

11. If we want to book profits or simply take some money off the table or need the money for any purpose, then we shall sell some or all the stocks on List 13 immediately without waiting for any signal.

12. All investments are dealt with in accordance with the sell confirmation signal from the technical strategy.

Akash: What if the company has gone off the Main List but the technical strategy does not give a sell signal at all? In such a case, we may end up being invested in a company long after it has been eliminated from the new Main List.

Lucky: If such a situation arises, we do not need to do anything extra. We stay invested until we get a sell signal.

There is a reason for this. You must understand that prices in the stock market are based on estimated earnings. It may so happen that a company posts bad results in one quarter and is therefore eliminated from the Main List, but investors may feel that there is potential upside and do not sell their holdings. In such a case, we do not want to miss the move up and should hold on till there is a confirmed sell signal. The company may again post good results and come back into the Main List. So we save ourselves the trouble of getting in and out of a good stock.

Meghna: What if the company has gone off the Main List and there is also a sell signal with the technical method? When do we buy it again?

Lucky: Once it has gone off the Main List and has been sold with the technical method, we shall not buy it again till it comes back on our Main List.

Akash: Why is this technical sell signal important? Is the fundamental method not good enough?

Lucky: It is not good enough by itself because the fundamental factors lag the market by some time. The latest fundamental data or news item is not known to us till the company informs the stock exchanges. In most cases, by then this data or news is already reflected in the stock price. Only, the investors do not know it. Informed people are already buying or selling the stock of the company based on such data or news. The technical charts can tell us the trend of the stock price in advance of the data or news as it is based on price and trading data provided by the stock exchanges, and not on fundamental factors.

Akash: How is it possible that informed people trade on unknown data?

Lucky: Because a lot of people, in close contact with the company, have information about sales, profitability and other issues being faced by the company before they are declared to the stock exchanges, and, hence, they are already trading in the stock on that basis before the news becomes public.

Meghna: But is that not illegal?

Lucky: Yes, it is, but nevertheless it is commonplace. So we have to account for it.

Akash: Can we shift investments from List 13 to List 55?

Lucky: Of course! When the special situation which warranted the shift to short term has changed, then we can regard any short term investment as long term by shifting the investment from List 13 to List 55.

But, before anything else, let me introduce you to the concept of technical charts. Charts are diagrams which map the price movement of any stock over time.

Akash: Okay, that makes sense. Let's talk about the technical factors.

19

Technical Factors

Lucky: In the technical strategy, we use technical charts to monitor stocks on the Main List, List 55 and List 13.

The reasons for their use are many. The first is that technical charts reflect market sentiment. We all know that market sentiment plays a huge role in the price of any stock. As these charts are made from the actual price and trading data, we can assume that they reflect all information, declared or undeclared, pertaining to a company and which the investor is generally not in a position to gauge. They also reflect the buying or selling of large investors. Hence, all things considered, they are pretty reliable indicators of the trend of the market.

Meghna: Is this complicated? Does this not require specialized knowledge?

Lucky: No, this is not complicated for investors. But it can become pretty complicated for traders as they deal with a large number of indicators. But, then, we are not traders. We only need to know whether the market is supporting the companies whose stocks we want to buy or have already bought.

Now, let's come to the technical chart itself.

It is a graphic representation of the stock price over a period of time, with the price represented on the y-axis (the vertical axis) and time on the x-axis (the horizontal axis). The price can be represented as a line, bars, and also in esoteric ways such as candlesticks. Basically, they all represent the price in different formats. The details which can be shown are the open, high, low and closing prices over a period of time. This time period can vary depending upon the usage of the chart. A daily or weekly chart means representation of price data per day or per week, respectively.

We can use a line chart for its simplicity. A line chart is one which plots only the closing price. But to make critical trading decisions, we use a bar chart (also called OHLC chart). because it gives more information than a line chart. We do not need to use the candlestick chart at all.

These charts are available for free at the website www.icharts.in/charts.html *(see* Appendix D). If we go to that website and enter the name of the company at the appropriate place, it will bring up a chart.

An alternative to this website is http://finance.yahoo. com (*see* Appendix E).

Now, charts can be of various time periods. We shall always use a daily time period chart for both short and long term investments. I shall explain both of these later.

The charts are messy and volatile. In its plain or raw form alone, a chart is not of much use to us. We shall add some tools, called indicators, to the chart to make it useable for us. These indicators help decipher the raw data of the market.

The indicators we shall use are called Moving Averages. A moving average is a plain average of data over a specific period of time calculated by a specific method. It is a value that represents the price data over a specified period. We can set this period as per our requirement. It is called "moving average" because it changes every time fresh price data is added, and is represented by a line of these changing values. This average can be a simple average or an exponential average based on the method of calculation. The exponential average gives continuous and more accurate values, hence we will use only exponential average. This is also called EMA. We do not need to go into the method of calculation.

We add two averages on the price chart by entering the value at the appropriate place on the website. One is a 13-period Exponential Moving Average (13 EMA), and the other is a 55-period Exponential Moving Average (55 EMA). These will be calculated on the closing prices. It may look like EMA (Close, 13) and EMA (Close, 55).

Akash: This is getting complicated. Can we do without this section?

Lucky: No, you cannot do without it. If you do not follow this, you would be worse off than if you did follow it. Also, as you will see, it is not difficult at all.

Now, if we have the price and the averages ready we can use them effectively.

We need one more window at the bottom of the screen. This is called volume. We can request this on the website.

This gives the volume actually traded every day and is plotted directly under the price pertaining to that day.

Meghna: So we have three things — the price chart, moving averages, and the volume.

Lucky: Yes. The price and moving averages appear in one window, and the volume in another window directly below it. It looks like Chart 19.1 which is the daily chart of the popular index — Nifty.

The black (red in later charts in the book) and grey (green in later charts) bars represent the price. A black (or red) bar indicates a lower close than the previous day's closing price. A grey (or green) bar indicates a higher close than the previous day's closing price. The two lines in the chart are the 13 EMA (black line) and 55 EMA (dotted line). The open, high, low and closing prices are indicated on the top of the chart window. The values of the 13 EMA and 55 EMA are indicated on the main chart window. The volume window is shown below the price window. (The page link is http://www.icharts.in/charts.html.)

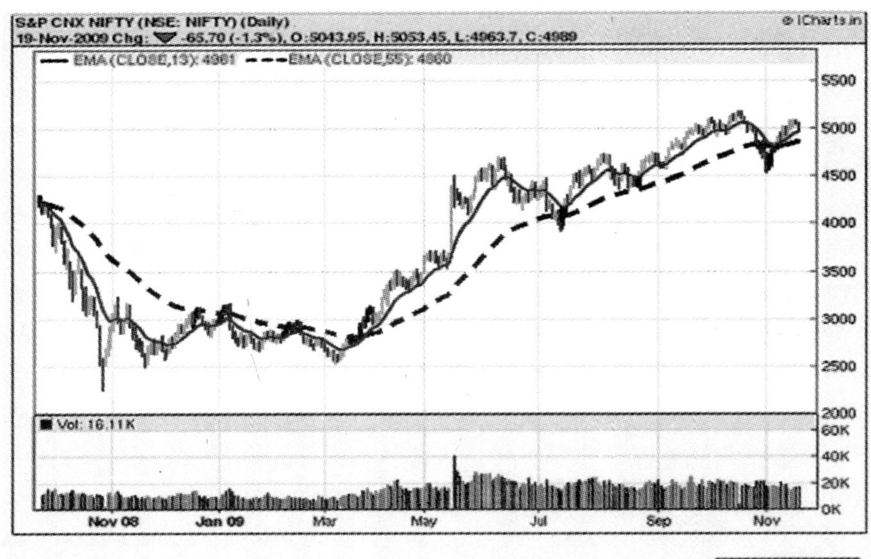

Chart 19.1: **Daily Chart of Nifty**

You will notice that in this chart the price is generally closer to the 13 EMA than the 55 EMA. At times, the price crosses below the EMAs moving downwards, and also the 13 EMA crosses above the 55 EMA moving upwards. We shall use these as our signals to confirm our trades. Note that this system will not work well for stocks whose price can be easily manipulated. These are typically medium and small sized companies where the floating stock (stock in public circulation) and average volume traded per day is low.

20

Technical Strategy

Meghna: Well, that does not seem so complicated now that you have explained it. So please describe your secondary method of investment.

Lucky: The secondary method is based on the technical factors which you have just seen. While this is not a fool-proof method, it gives us an advantage over using only the fundamental method both by helping us protect our capital and by giving us timely exit signals.

One of the chief advantages of this method is that of being able to gauge the market trend by analyzing charts of the main indices and also the major stocks they represent. The main indices may be manipulated by large investors thus creating an illusion of strength in the market, but no one can manipulate all the component stocks of the indices at the same time. It would be a good practice to see the charts of all the stocks of a major index, like the CNX Nifty, at least once a week to draw your own conclusions about the market's direction.

This is both a confirmation and a timing strategy, and works as follows:

1. Once the stock to be bought has been selected, we confirm this with the technical chart.

   The stock's price should be above its 13 and 55 EMAs, the 13 EMA should be higher than the 55 EMA, and both the averages should be rising.

   We should wait to confirm that the price remains above the averages for at least 2 to 3 working days — and then buy above the highest price of those 2 or 3 working days.

   Sometimes, especially during periods of sideways movement, there will be false signals of 13 EMA crossing the 55 EMA upwards. At such times it is advisable to do the following — (a) check the charts of the main index like the Nifty; (b) check the charts of some of the large cap companies even if they are not in the Main List; and (c) check whether the price rise is confirmed by high volumes. Then take a decision to buy the stock only if the general trend is upward.

2 We should aim to buy at a price as close to the 55 EMA as possible. This is for the purpose of protection of our capital. We should not buy a stock at a price which is more than 10% higher than the value of its 55 EMA. This is our limit price. All investments shall be included in our List 55.

3 A special situation may arise when the market is rising rapidly and the price of the stock is beyond our limit price. In such cases, we may still buy the stock as close to its 13 EMA as possible, and treat such investments

as short term investments. Such investments shall be included in our List 13.

4 Daily time period charts of stocks of all companies on the Main List must be checked every week to note the position of the price, 13 EMA, and 55 EMA. Daily time period charts of all investments, i.e. stocks on both List 13 and List 55, must be checked every day, or at least once every two or three days.

5 If the stock price is much higher than its 13 and 55 EMAs, and the 13 EMA is much higher than the 55 EMA itself, and your investment is also showing a good profit, you may consider booking some profits, as the price generally converges towards the averages.

6 For all investments on List 55, when the price crosses below the 55 EMA moving downwards (also referred to as the 55 EMA downward crossover), it may be time to sell the stock. We shall sell the stock if the price falls below the 55 EMA by more than 10%. Calculate the 10% from the day the price first closes below the 55 EMA.

7 If a stock which continues on the Main List is sold, we may buy it again if it re-qualifies.

8 We shall consider selling a stock on List 13 when its price crosses below the 13 EMA moving downwards (also called the 13 EMA downward crossover). We shall sell the stock if *both* the price falls below the 13 EMA by more than 5% *and* if the 13 EMA itself is falling.

9 If the stock is shifted from List 55 to List 13, and we find that the 13 EMA downward crossover has already taken place, then we sell that stock immediately.

Meghna: Suppose the price is greater than our limit price, why should we wait to buy the stock?

Lucky: This is to conserve capital. We should wait because the market may be in a euphoric mood. Volatility may be high. We must protect our capital at all times even if it means that we buy it at a higher price later but nearer the 55 EMA. You must also realize that these instances will be few and far between, but the rules are set as per the general situation. You may improvise a bit if you want.

Akash: How can we improvise in such a case?

Lucky: If the stock price is much higher than our limit buying price and you still wish to buy it as you feel that the price is not going to come down, you may still buy it as a short term investment.

Akash: Would you sell a stock based on the technical chart even if the company is doing well?

Lucky: Yes, I would sell even if the company is doing well. This is a simple stop loss mechanism which will allow you to exit companies where some factor may be going against the price of the stock. If the company is actually doing well, we can enter it again when we get confirmation from the chart.

Akash: Should we wait to buy the stock if the company is on the Main List but the 13 EMA is below the 55 EMA?

Lucky: We will not buy the stock if the 13 EMA is below the 55 EMA because the market is not confirming the buy. In such a case, we shall wait for the upward crossover.

Akash: How do we check for higher volume?

Lucky: On our chart, the window below the price line chart shows the total volume of trades which took place on each day. This is represented by bars. Taller bars mean higher volume.

Akash: Tell us how to interpret volume data.

Lucky: Right. Proper interpretation of volume is important because it gives us clues to the stock's future price movement. Volume, at any point in time, may be high, normal or low. This concept of high, normal or low volume on a particular date is relative to volumes seen in the previous two to three months.

The price of a stock is a function of its demand and supply at any time. If the volume is high but the stock's price remains approximately the same, it means demand equals supply at that price. If the price moves up with high volume, it means that the demand is greater than its supply, and the price is likely to go up further till the point when the demand will equal supply.

If the price moves down with high volume, it means its supply is greater than the demand and the price will move down further till the point when the supply will equal demand.

So, naturally, we should be interested when price is moving up with volume, and should be careful when price moves down with volume.

Now if the price moves up with low volume, it means that there are few buyers at those prices and so the price is likely to fall back.

Prices can often move down with low volume and this does not convey any special meaning.

Likewise, price movement, up or down, with normal volume does not convey any special meaning.

So we should be careful when we are getting a buy signal but the volumes are low.

Meghna: Is there a way to compare charts of different companies?

Lucky: Bravo! I was not expecting this question from you at this stage. Yes, charts of different stocks may easily be compared. In some charts, prices will rise steadily with the moving averages. These are stable charts. In other charts, prices will be volatile and move quickly up and away from the averages, and then converge towards them rapidly. These are volatile charts. There will be yet other charts where the prices will not be rising at all but moving sideways or down, even as the price of the benchmark index moves up. These are the underperforming charts.

We want to invest in companies whose charts are stable, and even in some companies whose charts are volatile. But please remember that when investing in companies whose charts are volatile, we should be quick to book profits. We should not invest in companies whose charts are underperforming. If we have already invested in such a company, we should exit quickly.

Meghna: Isn't all this difficult to do?

Lucky: Believe me; it's very easy once you get the hang of it.

Akash: Do we always wait for the 55 EMA downward crossover to happen before we sell the stock?

Lucky: Generally, yes. But in Phase 3 of the economic cycle there can be a situation when one is feeling that the market is too high or that there is too much euphoria. Then you can sell much earlier using the 13 EMA downward cross-over.

Akash: When you say "book some profits", what is the exit point?

Lucky: Booking profits may be done at any time at the current market price. It is like achieving a financial goal rather than waiting for a technical sell signal. I would generally sell half my shares if I am getting more than a 25% to 30% return.

Meghna: What is the reasoning for such an entry and exit system?

Lucky: The reason for this system is that we do not have to depend on anyone or anything else but the market to time our entries and exits. Also, we do not want to be caught on the wrong foot and neither do we get wedded to any particular stock.

Akash: Does this system work for all stocks?

Lucky: This system works best for stocks which have a reasonably good volume of activity. It does not work well for stocks which are prone to manipulation. Hence, we avoid stocks which are not popular.

Meghna: Can I use only the technical method and not the fundamental method?

Lucky: It is advisable to use both but if you are sure about the companies in which you want to invest, it is possible to use only the technical method.

Akash: Do we use only the daily time period chart in the cross-over system?

Lucky: Yes, we use only the daily time period chart in the cross-over system for both long and short term investments.

Meghna: What do you mean when you say "long term" and "short term"?

Lucky: By long term we generally mean 6 to 24 months, and by short term, we mean 1 to 6 months. Ideally, we would like to invest only for the long term but in times of uncertainty, i.e. when we are unsure of the phase of the economic cycle, or when there are circumstances which make us wary of investing, we may treat the investments as short term. By doing this, we shall be quicker to book profits or cut losses. We may, at any time, switch our gear from long to short term, or short to long term by just switching the method of exit.

Akash: Does the percentage of money in short and long term investments change as per the phase of the economic cycle?

Lucky: Great question!! Yes, the percentage of money in long and short term investments does change. In the initial part of Phase 1 of the economic cycle when we are uncertain of the economy and markets, as well as in the latter part of Phase 3, when we suspect that the economy may stop growing, we would generally want to book profits. Hence the percentage of money in short term investments would tend to increase at those times. In Phase 2, the investments would be mostly long term and the greater percentage of money would be in long term investment. In phases 4 and 5, the system may not let us enter the market.

Akash: Wow! This system allows us to be dynamic in approach as the situation demands.

Lucky: Yes, that's the beauty of it. With very little effort and cost, we can invest as well as the professionals. In fact, I would add that we can do better than most professional investors. Let me print some charts for you to understand the strategy (Charts 20.1 to 20.4).

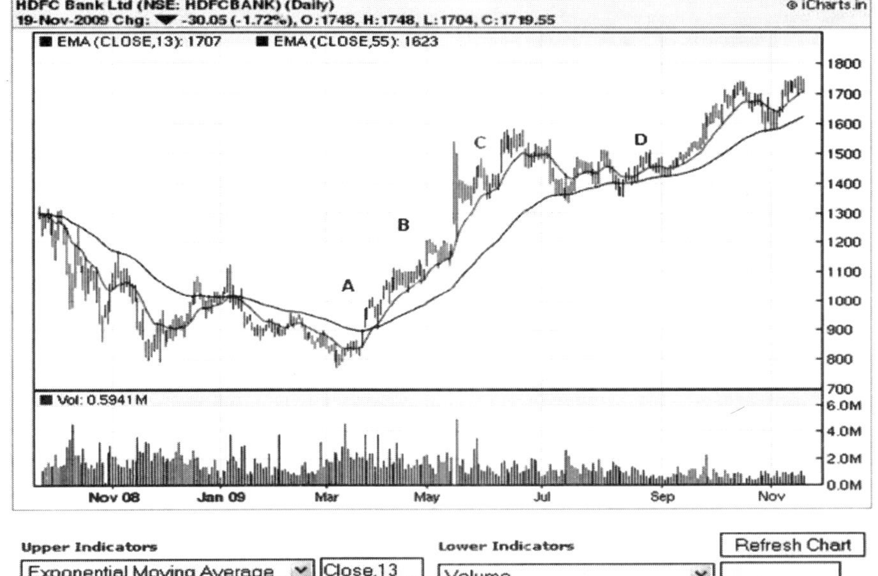

Chart 20.1: **HDFC Bank**

Point A at approximately ₹1,000 represents an area where there is a buying opportunity. Point B at approximately ₹1,100 represents an area where there is a "special situation" short term investment opportunity. Point C represents an area where buying should be avoided as it is too far away from the averages. Point D at ₹1,500 represents a second buying opportunity where the 13 EMA did not cross below the 55 EMA from above but came close to it, and then began to rise again.

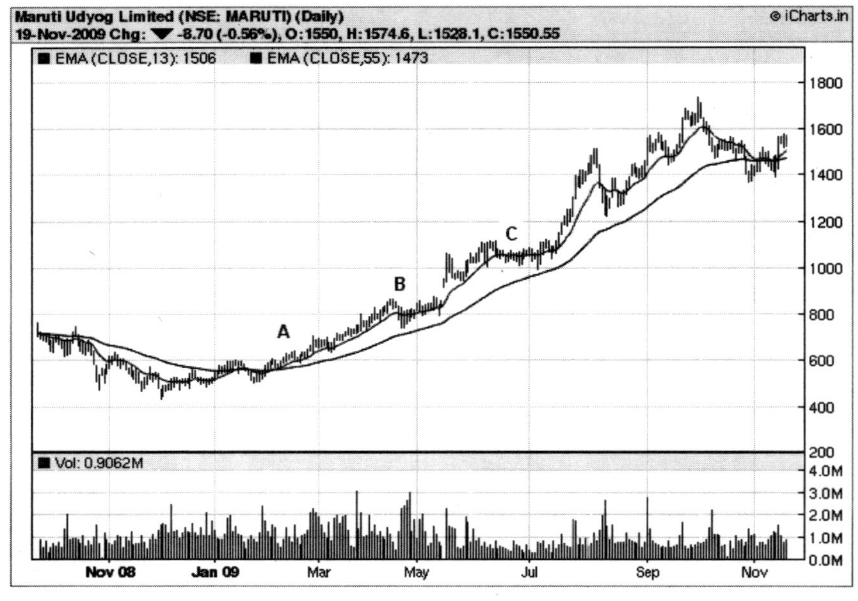

Chart 20.2: **Maruti Suzuki**

Point A represents an area where there is a buying opportunity. Point B represents an area where there is a "special situation" short term investment opportunity. At point C, the price does remain below the 13 EMA for some time. So there is a downward crossover but the 13 EMA is not falling. Hence there is no exit.

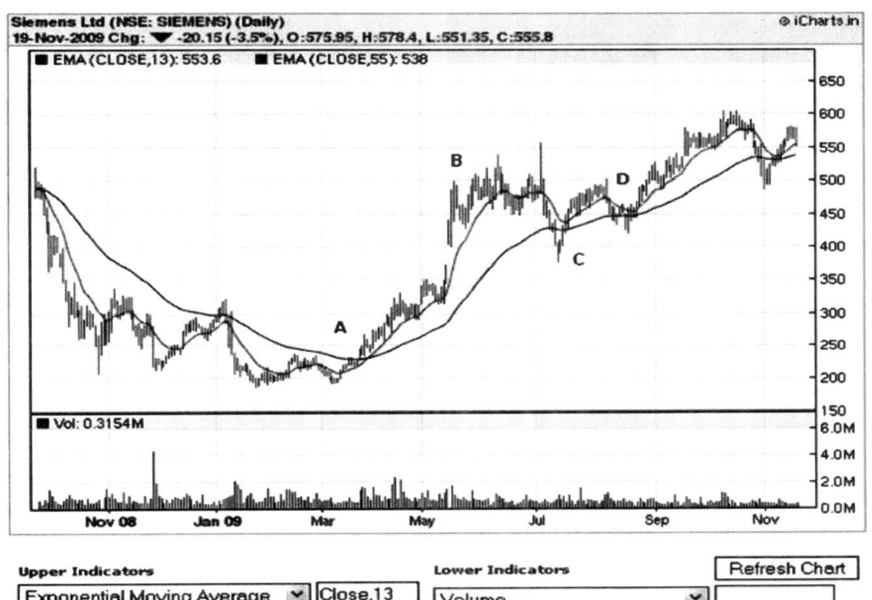

Chart 20.3: **Siemens Ltd.**

Point A at ₹250 represents an area where there is a buying opportunity. Point B represents an area which is abnormally far away from the averages. Even the 13 EMA is quite distant from the 55 EMA. At this point, one may consider booking profit. Point C is an area where the price has fallen below the 55 EMA, but our sell has not been triggered as per our "10% below 55 EMA" rule. Point D at ₹475 also represents a buy signal.

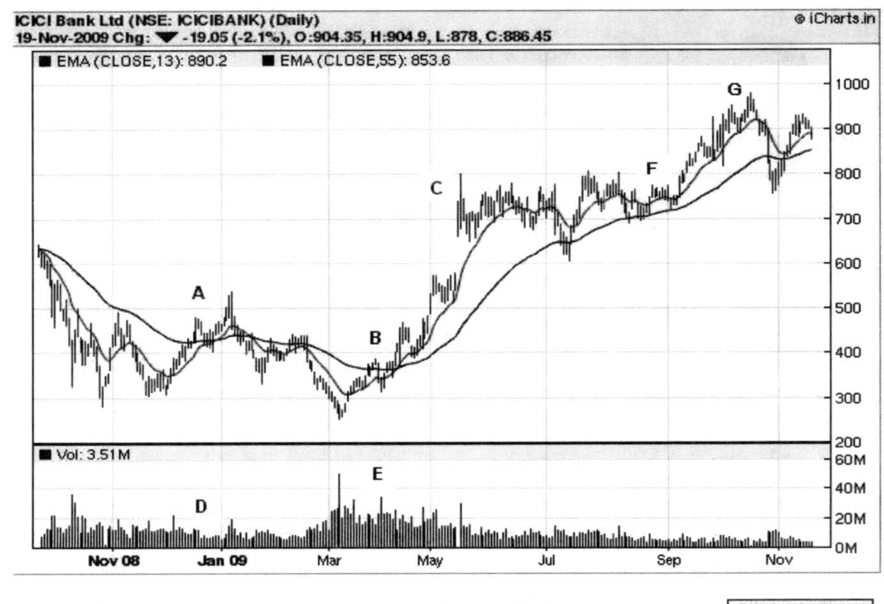

Chart 20.4: **ICICI Bank**

Point A is an area of a false buy signal as it is not supported by volume — see Point D in the lower window. Point B is the actual buying opportunity as it is supported by volume — see Point E in the lower window. Points C is a profit booking area being too far from the averages. The points F and G are again buying and profit booking opportunities.

21

Real Life Examples

Akash: Can you give us some real life examples on how we could have fared in the recent past using this system?

Lucky: Certainly, though in hindsight it may be difficult to recreate the Main List or ascertain which stocks we would have chosen from the list.

Meghna: Why don't we suggest some companies without really thinking much about them? Then we may be able to see the results randomly.

Lucky: Okay. But let's definitely use one assumption. This assumption is that in April 2010 it was almost certain that the world economic scenario would not be better 6 months down the road, especially with regard to the issue of sovereign risk of the European countries, high commodity prices and roll back of the stimulus package by the government.

Akash: What's sovereign risk?

Lucky: It's the risk that countries may not be able to honour their debt repayments.

Meghna: How do high commodity prices affect the economy?

Lucky: Commodities form the raw material for industry and, hence, high commodity prices mean higher costs.

Meghna: What was the stimulus package?

Lucky: This was the set of measures taken by the government to support the economy during the economic downturn in 2008. These measures included reduction in excise duties of industrial goods. Once the economy began reviving, the excise duty cuts started being restored to the earlier levels.

Akash: Why should the government roll back the stimulus package?

Lucky: There are two reasons. The first is that the stimulus package led to the government spending much more than it was earning. This put pressure on the government's budget and released excess money into the system leading to a rise in inflation. The second reason is that it is not a normal state of affairs; the government cannot support business forever at the cost of other taxpayers.

Akash: Okay. Let's assume that in April 2010 it was almost certain that the world economic conditions would not be better 6 months down the road. How does such an assumption affect our investments?

Lucky: Once we assume this, we transfer all our investments from List 55 to List 13.

Meghna: Now I get it. You need to make this assumption so that you may exit quicker based on the 13 EMA downward crossover.

Lucky: Clever.

Meghna: Let me suggest a company — Ambuja Cement. Please consider the chart.

Lucky: Here it is (Chart 21.1). I am going to print this and write down the possible trades just under the chart.

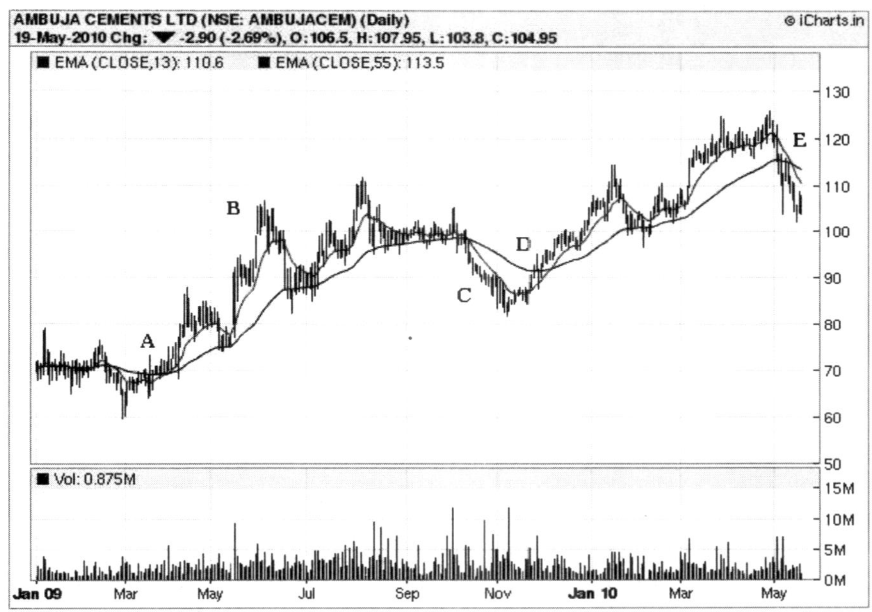

Chart 21.1: **Ambuja Cements Ltd.**

- 1st transaction — buy at A at ₹75 on the upward crossover.
- 2nd transaction — book some profit at B by selling half the quantity at ₹100, when the price was quite far from the averages.
- 3rd transaction — sell the balance at C at ₹87 per share on the 55 EMA downward crossover.
- 4th transaction — buy at D at ₹95 per share on the upward crossover.
- 5th transaction — sell at E at ₹114 per share on the 13 EMA downward crossover.

Meghna: Wow! This is awesome. How much profit would we have made?

Lucky: Suppose we bought 100 shares, then our initial investment was ₹7,500. You can easily do the math. We make a profit of ₹1,850 on the first set of transactions and ₹1,900 on the second set of transactions. A total of ₹3,750 on an investment of ₹7,500. That is a cool 50% in about 14 months.

Akash: Sounds too good to be true. Let's take a company which has not done too well, say, DLF.

Lucky: Of course, not all investments are going to do equally well, and we should consider all types of investments. Here is the chart of DLF Ltd. (Chart 21.2). You will see that we did not lose even here. In fact, we made a nice profit.

Let me also show you the charts of some of my favourite companies in the pages ahead (Charts 21.3 to 21.5).

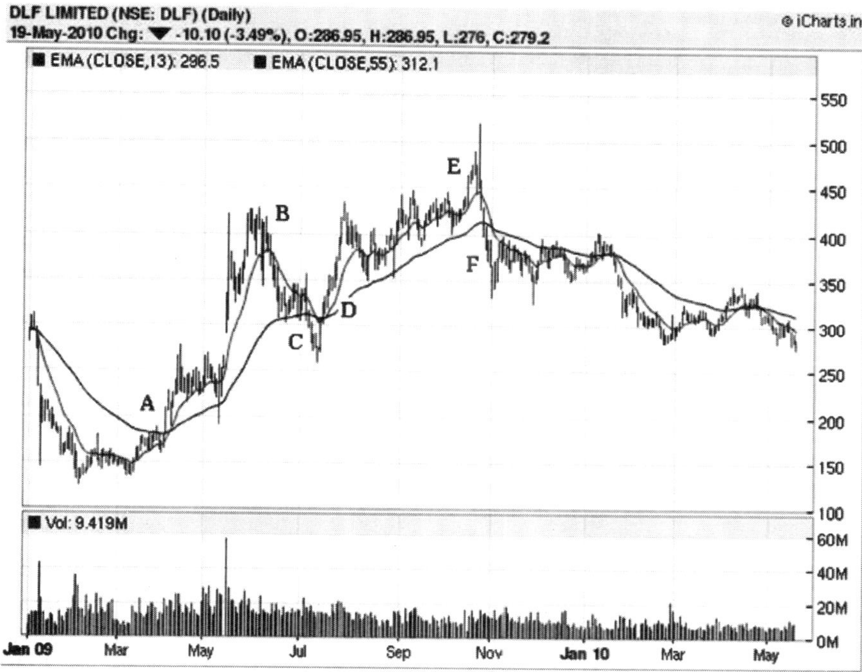

Chart 21.2: **DLF Ltd.**

- 1st transaction — buy at A at ₹200 on the upward crossover.
- 2nd transaction — sell half quantity at B at ₹400 when price moved quite far from the averages.
- 3rd transaction — sell balance at C at ₹275 on the 55 EMA downward crossover.
- 4th transaction — buy at D at ₹325 on the upward crossover.
- 5th transaction — sell half the quantity at E at ₹450 when the price moved quite far away from the averages.
- 6th transaction — sell balance at F at ₹380 on the 55 EMA downward crossover.
- There is no transaction beyond November 2009.

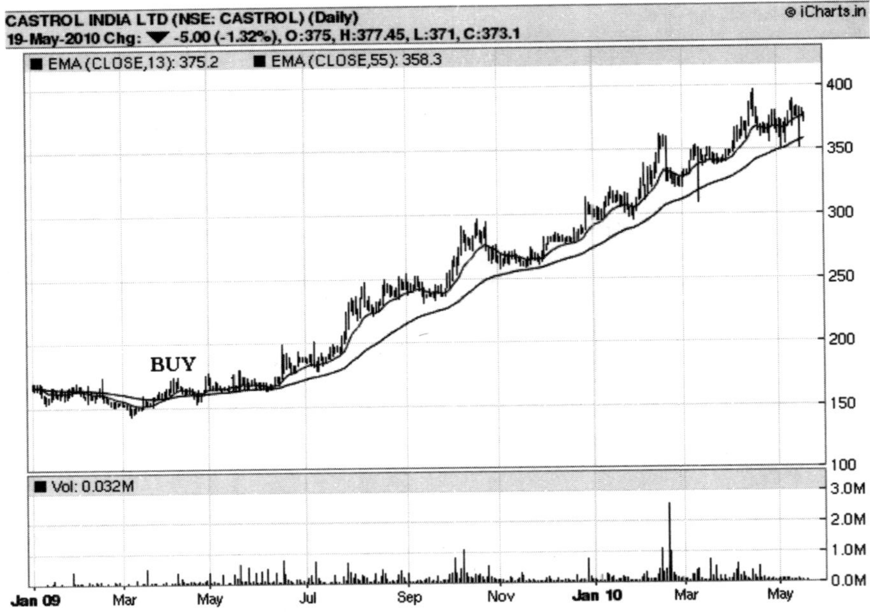

Chart 21.3: **Castrol India Ltd.**

Buy at ₹175 in April 2009 and still be in the trade at the time of the book's writing in May 2010 when the price was ₹375.

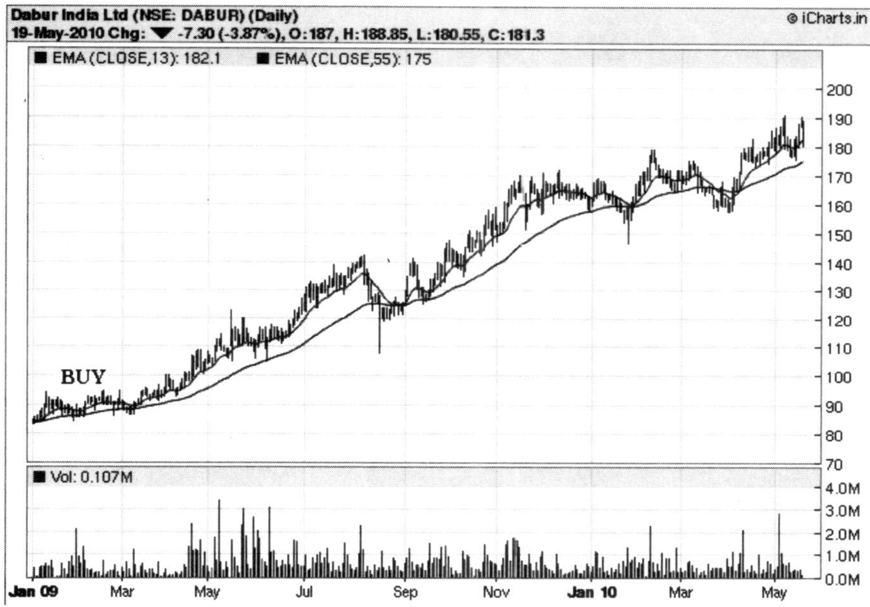

Chart 21.4: **Dabur India Ltd.**

Buy at ₹95 in February 2009 and still be in the trade at the time of the book's writing in May 2010 when the price was ₹180.

Meghna: Amazing. Those are huge profits of over 100%. I never thought it could be so simple for people like me.

Lucky: It is simple enough if you follow the rules. Let me warn you, though, that there are losses to be borne as well if you do not choose the right stocks.

Chart 21.5: **Titan Industries Ltd.**

Buy at ₹900 in May 2009 and still be in the trade at the time of the book's writing in May 2010 when the price was ₹2,300.

Did you notice that the three illustrations I chose — Castrol India, Dabur India and Titan Industries — have superb managements? Their products are well established and recognized all over India.

Akash: By God! I never thought of it in that way. I see what you are getting at. You have chosen the stocks which would have sailed through the elimination rounds under the qualitative factors.

Lucky: You are smart. Yes, and the results are there for you to see — great profits.

22

Critique and Conclusion

Lucky: So, what do you say? What is your first reaction now that we have discussed the complete Armchair Investing strategy? Have you been able to spot any flaws?

Akash: I think it's practical.

Meghna: I don't think it's going to be that simple to use.

Lucky: It will be once you get used to the exercises. But let me criticize the system myself.

The system is basically one which uses historical data to select companies, and then technical charts to invest and sell. This is its description in a nutshell.

But, we know that prices are a reflection of the future and not the past. So why don't we have a system in which we can also make estimates of future earnings, price the stocks accordingly, and then make investment decisions?

The answer to this is ignorance. We do not know how to make the correct estimate of any one company's future profits, let alone hundreds of them. We also cannot predict future interest rates. We cannot estimate future money flow. We cannot foresee upcoming technology and market changes. We cannot emulate those hundreds of factors which go into the investment decisions of thousands of investors on any single day.

And what if we are able to achieve the impossible? What if we are able to correctly estimate the future earnings of a company? But what if the largest shareholder of the company gets his math wrong and begins to sell his stocks? Then what? We shall be wiped out mercilessly due to the mistake of another.

I would rather be ignorant, follow the market and make decent money rather than try to be extra intelligent and get wiped out.

Akash: What if we find that we have missed the bus, and the good investment opportunities have gone?

Lucky: Do not fret. Be patient. There are corrections in all upward trending markets at least two or three times in a year, when prices converge towards the averages. When the prices begin to move up again after such corrections is the time to buy. It may be that we shall have to buy at higher prices but the risk of loss becomes quite low. Protection of capital is as important, if not more important, than profits.

Akash: Should we begin to invest as per these methods?

Lucky: Investment is about discipline but it also about controlling emotions tied to success, failure, loss and profit.

Theoretical study can never replace the actual thing. Begin with a small sum of money and then increase the amount if you feel comfortable.

Meghna: Thanks, we will certainly begin in a small way.

Lucky: Yes, try to build confidence in yourself and in the system. It is always easier to go into deeper fundamental issues regarding the economy, industries and companies, but we shall deal with this at another time. For now, this is absolutely fine.

Akash: Yes, I already feel confident that I can do this and perform better than I used to earlier.

Lucky: You definitely will. It is true everywhere, but never more so in the investment world — there is no free lunch. I can add another one to that — show me a guy who loves free advice, and I will show you a sucker whose money and he will soon be parted.

Meghna: Thanks a ton for the great lessons! I enjoyed every minute of it!

Lucky: Thanks for your time, and confidence in me. Have fun while investing! Let me celebrate the moment with a small poem — Luckyspeak (***see*** next page).

Luckyspeak

Money is serious, but money can be fun,

You can find it on the road, or it can be won.

It can multiply fast; it can vanish at one go,

But the best way to earn it is smooth, steady and slow.

Equity is the answer, come and join the game,

And if you use your common sense, your life will never be the same.

Debt, no doubt, is great; cash is even better,

But if the new Toyota tempts you; invest in equity and then go get her.

But, is equity risky? Sure, but then so is life,

Even crossing the road or fighting with your wife.

Minimize, minimize the risk; use your imagination,

There are rules to follow, give me your concentration.

Invest only for the long term, a couple of years at least,

Fear is an animal, greed is a beast.

If you lose your shirt, do not fret and fume,

Research your investment, before you assume,

That your choice is the star, which is going to shine bright,

Six out of ten, my dear friend, will be just about right,

To fulfill your dreams, your every desire.

23

Armchair Investing – Step-by-Step Summary

Chapter 1 – Why Invest in Stocks?

Stocks give a superior return when compared with other asset classes.

Risk is a function both of the investor's knowledge of investment rules and of the investment itself.

The amount of money that should be invested in stocks depends on the investor's loss bearing capacity, and this is different for each investor.

Part 1: Understanding the Quantitative Factors

Chapter 2 – Balance Sheet

The Balance Sheet of any company comprises of Liabilities (the source of funds) and Assets (the application of funds).

At any time the Liabilities equals the Assets:

- Liabilities = Share Capital + Reserves + Current Liabilities
  - Share Capital + Reserves = Shareholders' Funds
  - Current Liabilities = Sundry Creditors + Provisions
- Assets = Fixed Assets + Investments + Current Assets
  - Current Assets = Sundry Debtors + Stocks + Advances + Cash and Bank Balances

Chapter 3 – Profit and Loss Account

The Profit and Loss account of any company comprises of its Income and Expenditure over a period of time, typically one year.

- Total Income = Sales + Other income
  - Net Sales = Sales – Excise
  - Other Income = Income not related to operations but received regularly + Extraordinary income
- Total Expenditure = Cost of Goods Sold + Other Expenses
  - Other Expenses = Expenses not related to operations but spent regularly + Extraordinary expenses
- Profit before Depreciation, Interest & Tax (PBDIT) = Total Income – Total Expenditure
- Profit before Tax (PBT) = PBDIT – Depreciation – Interest
- Profit after Tax (PAT) = PBT – Tax
- Adjusted PAT = PAT – Extraordinary income + Extraordinary expenditure

Chapter 4 — Cash Flow Statement

The Cash Flow Statement of a company comprises of three parts — Cash from Operations + Cash from Investing activities + Cash from Financing activities. It gives the flow of cash in the business.

The most important section relates to Cash from Operations. Cash from Operations gives the flow of cash in the operations part of the business and reveals how much cash the company has been able to generate from its operations.

The Cash from Operations is not the same as the Cash Profit which companies normally advertise.

Cash from Operations can be substantially different from Net Profit.

Chapter 5 — Financial Ratios

- Operating Profit Margin (OPM) = (PBDIT – Other Income) × 100 ÷ Net Sales

OPM measures the efficiency of operations and is also a good comparison tool between different companies in the same industry.

- Return on Capital Employed (ROCE) = (Adjusted Net Profit ×100) ÷ (Shareholders' Funds + Debt)

ROCE measures efficiency of a company in its usage of capital.

- Return on Net Worth (RONW) = Adjusted Net Profit × 100 ÷ Shareholders' Funds

RONW is a measure of the return generated on the Shareholders' Funds. It is a tool used by investors to compare the return from the company's stock with the opportunity cost of their funds.

Chapter 6 — Some Common Financial Terms

Face Value (FV) of a share is its nominal value or the value at which it was issued by the company.

- Share Capital = Number of shares issued × Face Value

Dividend is a payout of profits in cash. It is calculated on the FV. Tax is payable on dividend as soon as you receive it.

Bonus is a payout of profits in the form of a company's shares. It is done by capitalizing free reserves (which means transferring some amount from the reserves to the share capital). Tax is payable on bonus shares only when you sell them.

- Price / Earnings (P/E) Ratio = Price ÷ Earning per share (EPS)

The P/E ratio is one of the most important ratios as it forms the basis of share valuation. It is also one of the popular gauges of investor confidence.

Trailing Twelve Months (TTM) relates to the financial data of a company for the latest 4 quarters combined as opposed to a fixed financial year. It is actually the most current data available.

Part 2: Understanding the Qualitative Factors

Chapter 7 – Management

A company's Management is the single most important criterion for investing in a company's stock.

An investor-friendly, honest and efficient management is the best type of management which an investor can desire. An efficient but non-investor friendly management is not preferred.

Some company managements resort to insider trading. This means that they, or persons close to them, trade in their company's stock on the basis of price sensitive information relating to the company which they are aware of as insiders but which is unknown to investors at large.

Individual investors are generally the last people to know of price sensitive information. Hence, there is a need for them to be extra careful.

Chapter 8 – Nature of Business

Businesses may be classified into two types — commodity type and non-commodity type.

Commodity type businesses are those whose products sell at attractive prices, whereas non-commodity type businesses are those whose products sell on attractive quality.

Non-commodity type businesses command a premium. They are the preferred investment category.

Chapter 9 — Debt

Debt is either good or bad depending on who is doing the borrowing.

Generally, companies with a great ROCE and who can manage capital efficiently have a great friend in debt. They leverage their business by borrowings leading to very good profitability.

Generally, companies with a poor ROCE cannot manage capital efficiently and should stay away from huge debt. In bad times, a huge debt can lead to serious issues.

Investors should gauge the debt management capability of a company before investing in it.

Chapter 10 — Diversification and Expansion

Diversification is the term given to the activity of a company going into an unrelated area of business. Generally, this leads to disaster in most cases.

Expansion, on the other hand, is the term given to the activity of a company going into a related area of business. This can lead to high growth and good profitability.

In these globalised times, expansion of markets has become imperative for all good companies.

Part 3: Important Concepts in Investing

Chapter 11 — Economic Cycle

Economies move in cycles. Each economic cycle broadly consists of six phases. Each phase has it own peculiar characteristics. It is a reality that markets move in consonance with these phases. An investor would do well to follow and ascertain the ongoing phase of the economic cycle and make investment decision accordingly:

Phase 1: The early stage of a growing economy. Some growth with some uncertainty. Interest rates bottom out. Sectors which do well are auto and technology.

Phase 2: The middle stage or best stage of a growing economy. All round growth. Interest rates are rising. Sectors which do well — raw materials, services, capital goods.

Phase 3: The last stage of a growing economy. Some bad news, high inflation. Interest rates very high. Unknown stocks in the limelight. Sectors which do well — realty, oil, telecom.

Phase 4: The early stage of a declining economy. Interest rates are peaking. Central banks and governments act to stem the decline. Sectors which do well — pharma, FMCG , i.e. the defensive sectors.

Phase 5: The middle — and the worst — stage of the declining economy. Interest rates are falling. General hardship all around. Sectors which do well — utilities, banking.

Phase 6: The last stage of the declining economy. Some signs of revival. Interest rates are coming down. Sectors which do well — consumer durables, finance, retail.

The ideal investment strategy would be to invest in Phase 1 and exit in Phase 3.

Chapter 12 – Inflation, Money Flow and Behavioural Trend

Inflation is a measure of yearly price increase in commonly used items.

A healthy inflation, which is a little lower than the bank deposit rate, is good for the economy whereas a higher or lower inflation is bad for the economy.

Fiscal deficit is the excess of budgetary expenditure over income. A high fiscal deficit can lead to high inflation and is, therefore, is bad for the economy.

Money flow refers to the flow of money between countries and across asset classes. A good investor keeps a tab on where money is flowing to be able to take good investment decisions.

Behavioural study is the study of human behaviour in various situations, and their reaction to varied circumstances.

A phenomenon called a "bubble" often occurs in markets. This is a phenomenon in which investors behave irrationally to drive up stock prices as a reaction to rising prices rather than any inherent value. The reverse happens in falling markets.

These bubbles invariably burst and investors get terribly hurt financially.

Chapter 13 – Investment Rules and Tools

1. Never argue with the market.
2. Never buy a falling market. Always buy a rising market.
3. Buy only liquid stocks.
4. Never average a loss.

5. Believe in yourself. Do your own homework.
6. Never follow hot stock or tips.

Use tools to increase your awareness of the state of the economy, industries and companies. Do not believe rumours blindly. Evaluate them yourself.

Part 4: The Armchair Investing Set-up

Chapter 14 – Preparing List 1 with Annual Data

1. Begin with a list of liquid stocks like CNX 200.

   Classify the companies on the list based on Net Sales. Large companies are those whose Net Sales are higher than ₹5,000 crore; medium companies are those with Net Sales between ₹1,000 crore and ₹5,000 crore; and small companies are those with Net Sales between ₹200 crore and ₹1,000 crore. Ignore companies with Net Sales of less than ₹200 crore.

2. Large, medium and small companies need to have a RONW figure for the latest financial year of at least 10%, 15% and 20%, respectively. Eliminate companies which do not meet the standard.

3. Eliminate all companies whose Net Sales have decreased in the latest financial year as compared with the previous financial year.

This gives us our List 1.

Chapter 15 – Preparing List 2 with Current Data

1. Begin with List 1.
2. Eliminate all companies whose TTM Net Profit has fallen in comparison with the corresponding figure of the previous financial year.
3. Eliminate all companies whose latest Quarterly Net Sales or latest Quarterly Net Profit has fallen when compared with the corresponding figure of the previous financial year.
4. Large, medium and small companies need to have a promoter's stake of at least 15%, 25% and 35%, respectively. Eliminate companies which do not meet this standard. Promoter's stake should be ignored for large companies where there is no identifiable promoter, e.g. ITC, Larsen & Toubro, HDFC Ltd. and ICICI Bank.
5. Add all the stocks of the CNX Nifty which have been eliminated.

This gives us our List 2.

Chapter 16 – Preparing the Main List

1. Begin with List 2.
2. Grade companies according to different qualitative criteria in the following order:
    - Management;
    - Commodity type or Non-commodity type business;
    - Non transparent, complicated, glamorous, government dominated or labour intensive business;

- Operating Profit Margin and ROCE; and
- Popular index in which the company is included.

3. Eliminate companies based on the different criteria until you are left with 2 to 3 large, 1 to 2 medium, and 1 to 2 small companies in about 10 to 15 industries.

This is our Main List.

Chapter 17 — Keeping Track

1. Prepare a fresh Main List every quarter.
2. Note monthly closing price data for stocks of all companies on the Main List. Calculate the percentage change in the monthly closing prices.

Part 5: The Armchair Investing Strategy

Chapter 18 — Fundamental Strategy

Invest and remain invested so long as you feel that economic conditions six months down the road are going to be better than they are today.

Adhere to the following system:

1. Maintain monthly closing price tables for stocks of all companies on the Main List, and also calculate percent changes in closing prices.
2. Keep a track of the likely phase of the economic cycle through media input, awareness of economic conditions and also monthly closing price data.

3. Limit exposure in any single industry or sector to 10%-15% of the portfolio.

4. Allocate 70% or more of the funds to large companies, and only 30% or less to medium and small companies.

5. Review the Main List every quarter.

6. Buy out performers and performers. Book profits in under-performers.

7. Initially, all investments are for the long term and this investment list is called List 55. In special situations some long term investments from List 55 will shift to the short term, and the list of all such short term investments is called List 13.

8. Shift the stock to List 13 when you wish to book profit; in "times of uncertainty"; and when you want to treat any stock as a short term investment.

9. If you want to book profits, or if funds are required, you may also sell stocks on List 13 without waiting for any sell signal.

10. All investments are dealt with in accordance with the sell signal from the technical strategy.

Fundamental analysis is good for selecting the right stocks to invest in, and technical analysis for confirmation of entry and exit signals.

Chapter 19 – Technical Factors

Technical analysis is a graphical study of price movement over time. It represents market action.

We use a minimal number of technical indicators as we are not traders.

A moving average is the plain average of data over a period of time. It is called moving average because everyday the time period shifts by one day and the data for the first day is replaced by data for the current day.

We use an Exponential Moving Average (EMA) for our investment purpose. The periods important in the Armchair Investing Strategy are 13 and 55, and their moving averages are 13 EMA and 55 EMA.

Out of the 13 and 55 EMAs, the 13 EMA is closer to the price most of the time.

Chapter 20 – Technical Strategy

This is a confirmation and timing strategy.

We use the following system:

1. Confirmation to buy a stock is obtained only if its price is above both its 13 EMA and 55 EMA, the 13 EMA is above the 55 EMA, and both averages are rising. Confirm whether the signal of 13 EMA crossing the 55 EMA upward is true or false by checking charts of the popular indices, popular stocks, and by volume.

2. Do not buy a stock at a price more than 10% higher than its 55 EMA value, as price tends to converge with the average at some point. This is our limit price, and is meant to protect our capital.

3. In a rapidly rising market, we may sometimes wish to buy at a price higher than our limit price. In such a case, buy the stock as near the 13 EMA as possible, and treat this as a short term investment.

4. Check daily time period charts for stocks of all companies on the Main List on a weekly basis. Check daily time period charts for all investments (List 55 and List 13) every day.

5. If the price is much higher than the 13 EMA, and the 13 EMA is much above the 55 EMA, and your investment is showing a good profit, book profits partially.

6. Sell a stock on List 55 when the price moves downwards and crosses the 55 EMA from above (called 55 EMA downward crossover), and the price falls below the 55 EMA by more than 10%. The value of the 55 EMA should be taken on the day the price first closes below the 55 EMA.

7. Sell a stock on List 13 when the price moves downwards and crosses the 13 EMA from above (called 13 EMA downward crossover), and the price falls below the 13 EMA by over 5% and the 13 EMA itself is falling.

8. If a stock is shifted from List 55 to List 13, and the 13 EMA downward crossover had already occurred, sell immediately.

If the technical strategy gives a sell signal, we sell in all circumstances.

Price is a function of demand and supply. Volume gives us clues to future price movement. If the price rises with high volume, it is likely to go up further.

It is possible to compare charts. Charts may be stable, volatile or underperformers. We should buy only stable charts. We may buy some volatile charts but in such cases we should also look for quick exits. We should avoid underperformers.

Short term means 1 to 6 months; long term means 6 to 24 months. We can easily switch from long term to short term by changing our exit strategy.

Chapter 21 – Real Life Examples

It is important to gauge if the economy is going to be better or worse six months in the future than it is now. With this assumption, the investor may transfer his investments from List 55 to List 13.

For example, in April 2010, the Eurozone sovereign risk, high commodity prices and roll back of stimulus package by the Government of India forced the assumption that the economy would be under pressure.

The investment strategy works well randomly, but would work better if the stocks in which the investment is made is chosen from the list which conforms to the elimination process including great management and good products.

Chapter 22 – Critique and Conclusion

The system uses historical fundamental data to select stocks, and price / time data through technical charts to confirm entry and time exit.

The reason we do not use fundamental data alone is that we are unable to accurately assess economic data. Also, the fundamental data does not include any price changes as a result of investor sentiment.

Investment is all about discipline and controlling emotions tied to success, failure, fear and greed.

Afterword

Armchair Investing system is a method for investing in, monitoring, and then exiting the stock market. The aim is to make reasonable and not spectacular profits. At times, this system may not allow investment even in a number of blue chip stocks. But it is safe and consistent.

By all means you can alter the system but it is recommended only if you are a mature investor.

I am not implying that only my method will make profits. It is, however, a system which allows budding investors and those hard-pressed for time to invest with confidence and expectations of steady gains.

A number of you may not agree with these methods. I don't even for a moment claim that my method is the best; my only claim that I have myself employed it successfully.

Happy investing to all my investor friends!

Appendix A: How to Use www.nseindia.com

1. Go to www.nseindia.com
2. Go to "Products".
3. Under "Capital Market" choose "Indices".
4. Go to "About Indices".
5. Choose "CNX Nifty".
6. Choose "Download List of CNX Nifty Stocks".
7. For other indices, choose the required one from the column on the left side. Then choose the download option.

The site may also be used for financial information regarding companies listed on it.

CNX 200 companies (as on 6 February 2014):

Company Name	*Industry*
Amara Raja Batteries Ltd.	Automobile
Apollo Tyres Ltd.	Automobile
Ashok Leyland Ltd.	Automobile
Bajaj Auto Ltd.	Automobile
Bosch Ltd.	Automobile
Eicher Motors Ltd.	Automobile
Exide Industries Ltd.	Automobile
Hero MotoCorp Ltd.	Automobile
Mahindra & Mahindra Ltd.	Automobile
Maruti Suzuki India Ltd.	Automobile
Motherson Sumi Systems Ltd.	Automobile
MRF Ltd.	Automobile
Tata Motors Ltd.	Automobile
ACC Ltd.	Cement & Cement Products
Ambuja Cements Ltd.	Cement & Cement Products
Century Textile & Industries Ltd.	Cement & Cement Products
Grasim Industries Ltd.	Cement & Cement Products
India Cements Ltd.	Cement & Cement Products
Shree Cement Ltd.	Cement & Cement Products
The Ramco Cements Ltd.	Cement & Cement Products
UltraTech Cement Ltd.	Cement & Cement Products
Gujarat Fluorochemicals Ltd.	Chemicals
Pidilite Industries Ltd.	Chemicals
Tata Chemicals Ltd.	Chemicals
DLF Ltd.	Construction
GMR Infrastructure Ltd.	Construction
Housing Development and Infra-structure Ltd.	Construction

(Contd . . .)

Company Name	*Industry*
Indiabulls Real Estate Ltd.	Construction
IRB Infrastructure Developers Ltd.	Construction
Jaiprakash Associates Ltd.	Construction
Larsen & Toubro Ltd.	Construction
Oberoi Realty Ltd.	Construction
Punj Lloyd Ltd.	Construction
Sobha Developers Ltd.	Construction
Unitech Ltd.	Construction
Voltas Ltd.	Construction
Asian Paints Ltd.	Consumer Goods
Bata India Ltd.	Consumer Goods
Berger Paints India Ltd.	Consumer Goods
Britannia Industries Ltd.	Consumer Goods
Colgate Palmolive (India) Ltd.	Consumer Goods
Dabur India Ltd.	Consumer Goods
Emami Ltd.	Consumer Goods
Gitanjali Gems Ltd.	Consumer Goods
GlaxoSmithkline Consumer Health-care Ltd.	Consumer Goods
Godrej Consumer Products Ltd.	Consumer Goods
Godrej Industries Ltd.	Consumer Goods
Havell's India Ltd.	Consumer Goods
Hindustan Unilever Ltd.	Consumer Goods
I T C Ltd.	Consumer Goods
Jubilant Foodworks Ltd.	Consumer Goods
McLeod Russel India Ltd.	Consumer Goods
Shree Renuka Sugars Ltd.	Consumer Goods
Tata Global Beverages Ltd.	Consumer Goods
Titan Company Ltd.	Consumer Goods
United Breweries Ltd.	Consumer Goods

(Contd . . .)

Company Name	*Industry*
United Spirits Ltd.	Consumer Goods
Videocon Industries Ltd.	Consumer Goods
Adani Power Ltd.	Energy
Bharat Petroleum Corporation Ltd.	Energy
Cairn India Ltd.	Energy
Castrol (India) Ltd.	Energy
CESC Ltd.	Energy
GAIL (India) Ltd.	Energy
Gujarat State Petronet Ltd.	Energy
Hindustan Petroleum Corporation Ltd.	Energy
Indraprastha Gas Ltd.	Energy
Jaiprakash Power Ventures Ltd.	Energy
JSW Energy Ltd.	Energy
NHPC Ltd.	Energy
NTPC Ltd.	Energy
Oil & Natural Gas Corporation Ltd.	Energy
Oil India Ltd.	Energy
Petronet LNG Ltd.	Energy
Power Grid Corporation of India Ltd.	Energy
PTC India Ltd.	Energy
Reliance Industries Ltd.	Energy
Reliance Infrastructure Ltd.	Energy
Reliance Power Ltd.	Energy
Tata Power Co. Ltd.	Energy
Chambal Fertilizers & Chemicals Ltd.	Fertilisers & Pesticides
Coromandel International Ltd.	Fertilisers & pesticides
Rallis India Ltd.	Fertilisers & pesticides
UPL Ltd.	Fertilisers & pesticides

(Contd . . .)

Company Name	*Industry*
Allahabad Bank	Financial Services
Andhra Bank	Financial Services
Axis Bank Ltd.	Financial Services
Bajaj Finance Ltd.	Financial Services
Bajaj Finserv Ltd.	Financial Services
Bajaj Holdings & Investment Ltd.	Financial Services
Bank of Baroda	Financial Services
Bank of India	Financial Services
Canara Bank	Financial Services
Central Bank of India	Financial Services
CRISIL Ltd.	Financial Services
Dena Bank	Financial Services
Federal Bank Ltd.	Financial Services
HDFC Bank Ltd.	Financial Services
Housing Development Finance Corporation Ltd.	Financial Services
ICICI Bank Ltd.	Financial Services
IDBI Bank Ltd.	Financial Services
IDFC Ltd.	Financial Services
IFCI Ltd.	Financial Services
Indiabulls Housing Finance Ltd.	Financial Services
Indian Bank	Financial Services
Indian Overseas Bank	Financial Services
IndusInd Bank Ltd.	Financial Services
ING Vysya Bank Ltd.	Financial Services
Jammu & Kashmir Bank Ltd.	Financial Services
Karnataka Bank Ltd.	Financial Services
Karur Vysya Bank Ltd.	Financial Services
Kotak Mahindra Bank Ltd.	Financial Services
L&T Finance Holdings Ltd.	Financial Services

(Contd . . .)

Company Name	*Industry*
LIC Housing Finance Ltd.	Financial Services
Mahindra & Mahindra Financial Services Ltd.	Financial Services
Max India Ltd.	Financial Services
Oriental Bank of Commerce	Financial Services
Power Finance Corporation Ltd.	Financial Services
Punjab National Bank	Financial Services
Reliance Capital Ltd.	Financial Services
Rural Electrification Corporation Ltd.	Financial Services
Shriram City Union Finance Ltd.	Financial Services
Shriram Transport Finance Co. Ltd.	Financial Services
South Indian Bank Ltd.	Financial Services
State Bank of India	Financial Services
Syndicate Bank	Financial Services
UCO Bank	Financial Services
Union Bank of India	Financial Services
Vijaya Bank	Financial Services
Yes Bank Ltd.	Financial Services
Apollo Hospitals Enterprises Ltd.	Healthcare Services
ABB India Ltd.	Industrial Manufacturing
Bharat Electronics Ltd.	Industrial Manufacturing
Bharat Forge Ltd.	Industrial Manufacturing
Bharat Heavy Electricals Ltd.	Industrial Manufacturing
Crompton Greaves Ltd.	Industrial Manufacturing
Cummins India Ltd.	Industrial Manufacturing
Jain Irrigation Systems Ltd.	Industrial Manufacturing
Pipavav Defence and Offshore Engineering Company Ltd.	Industrial Manufacturing
Siemens Ltd.	Industrial Manufacturing
Sintex Industries Ltd.	Industrial Manufacturing

(Contd . . .)

Company Name	*Industry*
Suzlon Energy Ltd.	Industrial Manufacturing
Thermax Ltd.	Industrial Manufacturing
CMC Ltd.	IT
Financial Technologies (India) Ltd.	IT
HCL Technologies Ltd.	IT
Hexaware Technologies Ltd.	IT
Infosys Ltd.	IT
MindTree Ltd.	IT
MphasiS Ltd.	IT
Oracle Financial Services Software Ltd.	IT
Tata Consultancy Services Ltd.	IT
Tech Mahindra Ltd.	IT
Wipro Ltd.	IT
Hathway Cable & Datacom Ltd.	Media & Entertainment
Sun TV Network Ltd.	Media & Entertainment
TV18 Broadcast Ltd.	Media & Entertainment
Zee Entertainment Enterprises Ltd.	Media & Entertainment
Bhushan Steel Ltd.	Metals
Coal India Ltd.	Metals
Gujarat Mineral Development Corporation Ltd.	Metals
Hindalco Industries Ltd.	Metals
Jindal Steel & Power Ltd.	Metals
JSW Steel Ltd.	Metals
NMDC Ltd.	Metals
Orissa Min Dev Co Ltd.	Metals
Sesa Sterlite Ltd.	Metals
Steel Authority of India Ltd.	Metals
Tata Steel Ltd.	Metals

(Contd . . .)

Company Name	*Industry*
Aurobindo Pharma Ltd.	Pharma
Biocon Ltd.	Pharma
Cadila Healthcare Ltd.	Pharma
Cipla Ltd.	Pharma
Divi's Laboratories Ltd.	Pharma
Dr. Reddy's Laboratories Ltd.	Pharma
Glaxosmithkline Pharmaceuticals Ltd.	Pharma
Glenmark Pharmaceuticals Ltd.	Pharma
Ipca Laboratories Ltd.	Pharma
Lupin Ltd.	Pharma
Opto Circuits (I) Ltd.	Pharma
Piramal Enterprises Ltd.	Pharma
Ranbaxy Laboratories Ltd.	Pharma
Strides Arcolab Ltd.	Pharma
Sun Pharmaceutical Industries Ltd.	Pharma
Torrent Pharmaceuticals Ltd.	Pharma
Wockhardt Ltd.	Pharma
Adani Enterprises Ltd.	Services
Adani Ports and Special Economic Zone Ltd.	Services
Aditya Birla Nuvo Ltd.	Services
Container Corporation of India Ltd.	Services
Great Eastern Shipping Co. Ltd.	Services
Indian Hotels Co. Ltd.	Services
MMTC Ltd.	Services
Bharti Airtel Ltd.	Telecom
Bharti Infratel Ltd.	Telecom
Idea Cellular Ltd.	Telecom
Reliance Communications Ltd.	Telecom

(Contd . . .)

Company Name	*Industry*
Tata Communications Ltd.	Telecom
Page Industries Ltd.	Textiles
Raymond Ltd.	Textiles

Appendix B: How to Use www.bgse.co.in

1. Go to www.bgse.co.in.
2. Go to "Get Quote" and enter the name of the company.
3. Choose the company from the list which comes up.
4. Choose "Income Statement / Financial Ratios / Cash Flow".
5. Repeat from Step 2 by using the "Search Company" window from any page within the site.

The site may also be used for other financial information of companies and market news.

Appendix C: How to Use *Capital Market*

1. Buy *Capital Market* magazine. This magazine is available fortnightly.
2. Go to "Corporate Scorecard Sector".
3. Under "TTM", look at "TTM NP Var %" for growth in TTM Net Profit
4. Under "Latest Quarter", look at "Sales Var %" for growth in Sales.
5. Under "Latest Quarter", look at "NP Var %" for growth in Net Profit.
6. Look at "Prom Stk (%)" for figures on Promoter's stake.

Appendix D: How to Use www.icharts.in

All the charts used in this book were created using the website www.icharts.in. Here are the steps for creating such charts at www.icharts.in:

1. Go to www.icharts.in
2. Choose "Charts" in the left column (or go straightaway to www.icharts.in/charts.html).
3. Go to "Symbol" on the right side of the page and enter. If you do not know the symbol, then search using the "?" icon next to the "Symbol" window.
4. Period: Daily
5. Chart Size: Large
6. Untick Log Chart
7. Chart Type: OHLC
8. Predefined Date Range: 1 year

9. Upper Indicators — 1st line: Exponential Moving Average in first window, and "Close,13" in the adjacent window.
10. Upper Indicators — 2nd line: Exponential Moving Average in first window, and "Close, 55" in the adjacent window.
11. Upper Indicators — 3rd line: None
12. Lower Indicators — 1st line: Volume
13. Lower Indicators — all other lines: None
14. Choose "Refresh Chart".
15. Repeat from Step 1.

Appendix E: How to Use http://finance.yahoo.com

1. Go to http://finance.yahoo.com
2. Type in the name of the index or company in the "Quote Lookup" box.
3. Select from the options presented.
4. The web page will open up.
5. Select "Interactive" under the legend "Charts" in the column on the extreme left hand side of the page
6. The web page will open up.
7. Go to "Technical Indicators" in the headings row.
8. Select "Exponential Moving Average".
9. Type in "13" in Line 1 and "55" in Line 2. Then click on Draw.
10. Go to "Technical Indicators" in the headings row.

11. Check whether Volume is already ticked. If not, select it.
12. Go to "Chart Settings" in the headings row.
13. Under "Line Type", select "OHLC".
14. Repeat Step 12 three more times, each time doing the following — under "Chart Scale", select "Linear"; under "Chart Cursor", select "Crosshair"; and under "OHLC Values", select "On".
15. Under the chart, there is an option to select the time period. Select "1Y" (1 year).
16. The chart, as we require it, shall open up.
17. To see another chart, type the name in the "Get Chart" box, select the correct option. All factors for the same session remain as it is.
18. Repeat from Step 1 for the next session.

Index

ADITYA SHROFF is a self-taught fundamental analyst and a qualified technical analyst. He has been awarded the Chartered Market Technician designation by the Market Technicians Association, New York, USA. He analyses stocks, commodities and forex as part of his job as a fund manager. He is an avid investor who believes that common sense is the most important qualification required to invest successfully. He may be reached by email at aditya@shroffgroup.in

SELECT PRAISE

"This book brings out a simplified method of making money through stocks. A wonderful book that reveals the secret of gaining wealth through investment in the stock market."

S. Hajara, Chairman & Managing Director,
The Shipping Corporation of India Ltd.

"Wonderful book . . . hats off to such a lucid approach to the subject . . . the conversational style, lively anecdotes tagged with a 'lesson' have all made the book simple. It is sure to attract readers who are normally shy of the stock market."

N. Kamakodi, Managing Director & CEO,
City Union Bank Ltd.

"Delightful book on a methodical investment system for effective entries and timely exits. It also offers practical and interesting insights into the universe of intelligent investment through the anecdotes."

N. M. Borah, Chairman & Managing Director,
Oil India Ltd.

(Continued Overleaf)

"I greatly enjoyed reading the book . . . timely, useful and well written."

R. Seshasayee, Executive Vice Chairman, Ashok Leyland Ltd., former President of Confederation of Indian Industry.

"A very useful book in an easy and understandable conversational style."

P. R. R. Rajha, Chairman and Managing Director of Madras Cements Ltd.

"Most importantly . . . interesting, reader friendly and very educative."

B. K. Birla, Chairman of B. K. Birla Group of Companies including Century Textiles & Industries Ltd. and Kesoram Industries Ltd.

"Strategy to profit on the bourses."

Hindu Business Line